Leading Projects to Success: The Ultimate Project Management Handbook

Table of Content

1. Introduction to Project Management Success

- Overview of project management principles and the importance of leadership.
- The evolving role of the project manager in modern businesses.

2. Defining Project Goals and Objectives

- Setting SMART goals and aligning them with business strategy.
- How to communicate objectives to ensure team alignment.

3. Building the Perfect Project Plan

- Creating a solid project plan with timelines, resources, and milestones.
- Tools for creating effective project plans (e.g., MS Project, Asana).

4. Stakeholder Identification and Engagement

- Identifying key stakeholders and managing their expectations.
- Strategies for maintaining long-term stakeholder relationships.

5. Team Building and Leadership

- Leading diverse teams and fostering collaboration.
- Techniques for resolving conflicts and improving team dynamics.

6. Project Scope Management

- Defining and controlling project scope to avoid scope creep.
- Methods for renegotiating scope without derailing the project.

7. Risk Management and Mitigation

- Identifying, assessing, and mitigating risks throughout the project lifecycle.
- Using risk management software to stay proactive.

8. Budgeting and Cost Management

- Managing project budgets, cost estimation, and tracking expenses.
- Tracking budget variance and controlling costs in real-time.

9. Time Management and Scheduling

- Techniques for effective time management, including Gantt charts and critical path method (CPM).
- Leveraging time-tracking tools to monitor productivity.

10. Communication Planning and Execution

- Creating a communication plan and ensuring effective information flow.
- The role of regular check-ins and reporting in maintaining project momentum.

11. Change Management in Projects

- Handling project changes smoothly and managing resistance.
- Engaging stakeholders early to ensure buy-in for changes.

12. Resource Allocation and Management

- Optimizing resource use and managing resource constraints.
- Strategies for reassigning or reallocating resources efficiently.

13. Agile vs. Waterfall: Choosing the Right Approach

- Understanding when to use Agile, Waterfall, or hybrid methodologies.
- Case studies showing successful implementation of both methodologies.

14. Project Monitoring and Control

- Tools and techniques to monitor project progress and make necessary adjustments.
- Using key performance indicators (KPIs) to evaluate project health.

15. Problem Solving and Decision Making

- Approaches for solving project challenges and making key decisions.
- Collaborative problem-solving techniques to encourage team input.

16. Quality Management in Projects

- Ensuring project deliverables meet the required quality standards.
- Leveraging quality management frameworks like Six Sigma.

17. Handling Project Crisis and Recovery

- How to manage project crises and get back on track.
- Creating contingency plans for potential project disasters.

18. Closing Projects Successfully

- Steps for project closure, reviewing deliverables, and post-project evaluation.
- The importance of celebrating project successes with the team.

19. Lessons Learned and Continuous Improvement

- Capturing lessons learned and promoting continuous improvement for future projects.
- Implementing a formal process for documenting lessons learned.

20. The Future of Project Management

- Emerging trends in project management, such as AI, remote teams, and new technologies.
- How to stay relevant as a project manager in a changing environment.

Chapter 1: Introduction to Project Management Success

In today's fast-paced and competitive business environment, effective project management has emerged as a critical factor for organizational success. Projects—whether they are launching a new product, implementing a new system, or conducting research—require careful planning, execution, and monitoring. The ability to lead projects successfully not only determines the outcome of individual initiatives but also influences the overall health and growth of an organization.

Understanding Project Management

Project management is the discipline of planning, executing, and overseeing projects to achieve specific goals within defined constraints such as time, budget, and scope. It involves applying knowledge, skills, tools, and techniques to project activities to meet or exceed stakeholder expectations. A well-managed project ensures that resources are utilized efficiently, risks are mitigated, and the desired outcomes are achieved.

The Role of the Project Manager

At the heart of successful project management is the project manager, who serves as the leader and central point of communication for the project team and stakeholders. The project manager is responsible for:

- **Planning**: Developing a clear project plan that outlines objectives, deliverables, timelines, and resource requirements.
- **Execution**: Leading the team in carrying out project tasks and ensuring that everyone understands their roles and responsibilities.
- **Monitoring and Controlling**: Continuously tracking project progress, identifying potential issues, and making necessary adjustments to keep the project on track.
- **Communication**: Facilitating effective communication among team members and stakeholders to ensure alignment and transparency.

Importance of Leadership in Project Management

Successful project management is not just about following processes; it requires strong leadership. A project manager must possess a blend of technical skills, interpersonal abilities, and emotional intelligence to guide the team effectively. Key leadership qualities include:

- **Vision**: The ability to articulate a clear vision for the project and inspire the team to work towards it.
- **Decision-Making**: Making informed and timely decisions, especially when faced with challenges and uncertainties.

- **Conflict Resolution**: Addressing conflicts within the team promptly and effectively to maintain a positive working environment.
- **Adaptability**: Being flexible and open to change, as project requirements and external conditions may evolve over time.

Defining Success in Project Management

Success in project management can be measured through various criteria, including:

1. **On-Time Delivery**: Completing the project within the established timeline.
2. **Budget Adherence**: Managing project costs effectively to stay within the allocated budget.
3. **Quality of Deliverables**: Meeting or exceeding the quality standards and expectations set for the project outcomes.
4. **Stakeholder Satisfaction**: Ensuring that stakeholders are satisfied with the project's results and the process through which they were achieved.

However, success is not solely about achieving these metrics; it also involves fostering a positive project environment that encourages collaboration, innovation, and learning.

The Evolving Landscape of Project Management

The field of project management is continually evolving, influenced by factors such as technological advancements, globalization, and changes in organizational structure. Trends such as remote work, Agile methodologies, and digital project management tools have transformed how projects are planned and executed.

As we navigate this dynamic landscape, project managers must stay informed about emerging trends, adapt their approaches, and continuously enhance their skills to remain effective leaders.

Conclusion

In conclusion, project management success hinges on a combination of robust methodologies, effective leadership, and a commitment to continuous improvement. As we embark on this journey through the subsequent chapters, readers will gain insights into various aspects of project management, equipped with practical tools and strategies to lead their projects to success. Whether you are an aspiring project manager or a seasoned professional, this handbook aims to provide you with the knowledge and skills necessary to navigate the complexities of project management and achieve outstanding results.

Chapter 2: Defining Project Goals and Objectives

Defining clear and actionable project goals and objectives is a foundational step in successful project management. Without a clear direction, projects can quickly veer off course, leading to wasted resources, missed deadlines, and unsatisfied stakeholders. This chapter explores the importance of establishing project goals and objectives, the methodologies for defining them, and practical tips for ensuring alignment and clarity throughout the project lifecycle.

The Importance of Goals and Objectives

Goals and objectives provide a roadmap for the project. They serve several critical functions:

1. **Direction**: Goals establish the overarching purpose of the project, while objectives break this purpose down into specific, measurable components. Together, they guide the project team in their efforts.
2. **Motivation**: Well-defined goals and objectives can inspire and motivate team members by providing them with a clear understanding of what they are working towards.
3. **Measurement**: Goals and objectives are essential for measuring progress and success.

They enable project managers and stakeholders to evaluate whether the project is on track and whether it meets expectations.

4. **Communication**: Clearly defined goals and objectives facilitate effective communication among team members and stakeholders. They ensure everyone is aligned on the project's purpose and desired outcomes.

Differentiating Between Goals and Objectives

While often used interchangeably, goals and objectives have distinct meanings in project management:

- **Goals**: These are broad, high-level statements that define the overall purpose of the project. Goals provide a vision of what the project aims to achieve but are typically not measurable. For example, a goal might be "to improve customer satisfaction."
- **Objectives**: These are specific, measurable, achievable, relevant, and time-bound (SMART) statements that break down the broader goals into actionable steps. An objective related to the goal above could be "to increase customer satisfaction scores by 15% within the next six months."

Setting SMART Objectives

To effectively define project objectives, project managers should employ the SMART criteria:

1. **Specific**: Objectives should be clear and precise. Instead of saying, "Improve sales," a specific objective would be, "Increase online sales of product X by 20%."
2. **Measurable**: There should be a way to measure progress towards the objective. This could involve quantitative metrics (e.g., sales numbers, completion percentages) or qualitative metrics (e.g., customer feedback).
3. **Achievable**: Objectives should be realistic and attainable, considering the available resources, time, and capabilities of the team. For instance, setting an objective to double sales in one month may not be realistic.
4. **Relevant**: The objectives must align with broader business goals and be relevant to the project's purpose. Each objective should contribute meaningfully to the overall goal.
5. **Time-Bound**: Objectives should have a specific timeline for completion. This creates a sense of urgency and helps prioritize tasks. For example, "Complete the website redesign by December 15."

Involving Stakeholders in Goal Setting

Involving stakeholders in the process of defining goals and objectives is crucial for ensuring buy-in and alignment. Here are some effective strategies:

- **Conduct Workshops**: Organize workshops or brainstorming sessions with key stakeholders to discuss and define goals and objectives collaboratively.
- **Gather Input**: Use surveys or interviews to gather input from various stakeholders. Understanding their needs and expectations can help shape more relevant objectives.
- **Communicate Clearly**: Ensure that the goals and objectives are communicated clearly to all stakeholders. This transparency helps build trust and ensures everyone is on the same page.

Documenting Goals and Objectives

Once the goals and objectives have been established, it is essential to document them formally. This documentation serves as a reference point throughout the project and can include:

- A project charter that outlines the goals and objectives.
- A project plan that details how these objectives will be achieved, including timelines and milestones.

Regularly revisit and update this documentation as the project progresses to ensure it remains relevant.

Reviewing and Adjusting Goals and Objectives

As the project unfolds, circumstances may change, requiring adjustments to goals and objectives. Factors such as shifts in market conditions, stakeholder feedback, or unforeseen challenges may necessitate a reevaluation.

1. **Regular Check-Ins**: Schedule regular meetings to review progress towards objectives and discuss any challenges that may arise.
2. **Be Flexible**: Cultivate a mindset of adaptability within the team. Encourage openness to change and the willingness to adjust objectives when necessary.
3. **Feedback Loops**: Implement feedback loops that allow team members and stakeholders to share insights and suggest changes to goals and objectives.

Conclusion

Defining clear and actionable project goals and objectives is a vital step in the project management process. By following the SMART criteria and involving stakeholders in the goal-setting process, project managers can create a strong foundation for project success. Regular review and adjustment of these goals and objectives ensure that the project remains aligned with the evolving needs of the organization and its stakeholders.

Chapter 3: Building the Perfect Project Plan

A well-constructed project plan is the backbone of successful project management. It serves as a roadmap that outlines how a project will be executed, monitored, and completed. A solid project plan not only helps in managing resources and timelines effectively but also acts as a communication tool that keeps all stakeholders aligned. In this chapter, we will delve into the key components of a project plan, best practices for building one, and tools that can assist in the planning process.

The Importance of a Project Plan

The project plan is crucial for several reasons:

1. **Guidance**: It provides clear direction for the project team, detailing what needs to be done, by whom, and when.
2. **Alignment**: It aligns the expectations of all stakeholders by establishing a shared understanding of the project's goals, deliverables, and timelines.
3. **Resource Management**: It aids in identifying the resources required for the project, including human resources, materials, and budget, enabling effective allocation.

4. **Risk Management**: A comprehensive project plan includes risk assessments and mitigation strategies, helping to prepare for potential challenges.
5. **Performance Measurement**: The project plan establishes benchmarks and milestones against which progress can be measured.

Key Components of a Project Plan

A robust project plan should include several essential components:

1. **Project Scope Statement**: This defines the boundaries of the project, including what is included and excluded. A clear scope helps prevent scope creep, which can derail the project.
2. **Objectives and Goals**: Outline the specific objectives and goals defined in the previous chapter. These should be measurable and aligned with the project scope.
3. **Deliverables**: Clearly list the tangible and intangible outputs that the project will produce. Each deliverable should be linked to specific objectives.
4. **Timeline and Milestones**: Develop a project schedule that includes key milestones and deadlines. Gantt charts are often used to visualize project timelines and dependencies.

5. **Resource Allocation**: Identify the resources needed for the project, including team members, tools, and budget. Detail how these resources will be allocated over the project timeline.
6. **Risk Management Plan**: Document potential risks and their impact on the project, along with strategies for mitigation. This proactive approach can save time and resources later.
7. **Communication Plan**: Outline how communication will occur throughout the project, including meeting schedules, reporting structures, and communication tools.
8. **Quality Management Plan**: Define the quality standards and processes that will be used to ensure that deliverables meet expectations.
9. **Change Management Plan**: Establish a framework for handling changes to the project scope or objectives. This should include processes for approval and documentation of changes.

Best Practices for Building a Project Plan

When building a project plan, consider the following best practices:

1. **Involve Stakeholders Early**: Engage stakeholders in the planning process to gather insights and ensure that their needs and expectations are

19

considered. This fosters buy-in and reduces resistance.

2. **Be Realistic**: Set achievable timelines and resource allocations. Overly optimistic estimates can lead to frustration and project failure.

3. **Document Everything**: Maintain thorough documentation of the project plan, including all decisions, changes, and approvals. This creates a clear record that can be referenced throughout the project.

4. **Use Visual Tools**: Utilize visual tools like Gantt charts, flowcharts, and diagrams to illustrate project timelines, workflows, and relationships. Visual representations can enhance understanding and communication.

5. **Review and Revise**: Regularly review the project plan and make adjustments as necessary. Flexibility is key, as project requirements and conditions may change over time.

6. **Establish Accountability**: Assign specific tasks and responsibilities to team members, ensuring that everyone knows their roles and what is expected of them.

Tools for Project Planning

Various tools can facilitate the project planning process, including:

1. **Project Management Software**: Tools like Microsoft Project, Trello, Asana, and Monday.com allow teams to collaborate, assign tasks, and track progress in real-time.
2. **Gantt Chart Tools**: Software specifically designed for Gantt chart creation, such as Smartsheet or GanttProject, can help visualize project timelines and dependencies.
3. **Risk Management Tools**: Tools like RiskyProject or RiskWatch enable project managers to assess and monitor risks effectively.
4. **Documentation Tools**: Platforms like Google Docs or Confluence provide collaborative environments for documenting project plans and sharing them with stakeholders.

Communicating the Project Plan

Once the project plan is finalized, it is essential to communicate it effectively to all stakeholders. Consider the following strategies:

1. **Kickoff Meeting**: Organize a project kickoff meeting to present the project plan to the team and stakeholders. This is an opportunity to clarify roles, expectations, and project objectives.
2. **Distribute Documentation**: Share the project plan document with all stakeholders, ensuring they have access to the information they need.

3. **Regular Updates**: Schedule regular check-ins and status updates to keep stakeholders informed of progress and any changes to the plan.

Conclusion

Building the perfect project plan is a critical step in leading a project to success. By carefully outlining the project's scope, objectives, deliverables, timeline, and resource allocations, project managers can create a comprehensive roadmap that guides the team through the execution phase.

Chapter 4: Stakeholder Identification and Engagement

Successful project management requires not only a solid plan and clear objectives but also the active involvement of stakeholders. Stakeholders play a crucial role in shaping project outcomes, providing necessary resources, and influencing key decisions. In this chapter, we will explore how to identify stakeholders, assess their influence and interests, and engage them effectively throughout the project lifecycle. Understanding stakeholder dynamics is essential for fostering collaboration, ensuring support, and avoiding potential conflicts that could derail the project.

Understanding Stakeholders in Project Management

In the context of project management, **stakeholders** are individuals, groups, or organizations who have an interest in the project's success or failure. These parties can directly or indirectly affect the project's outcomes, or they can be affected by the project's success or failure. Stakeholders can range from internal team members to external clients, vendors, regulatory bodies, and even the public.

Key points to consider about stakeholders:

- **Internal stakeholders**: These include the project team, executives, department heads, and employees who are part of the organization managing the project.

- **External stakeholders**: These are entities outside the organization, such as clients, suppliers, regulatory authorities, investors, or end-users of the project's deliverables.

Step 1: Identifying Stakeholders

The first step in stakeholder management is to identify all relevant stakeholders early in the project. Missing key stakeholders or identifying them too late can lead to misalignment or overlooked requirements, ultimately jeopardizing the project.

Methods for Stakeholder Identification:

1. **Brainstorming with the Project Team**: Engage the project team in a brainstorming session to list potential stakeholders. Consider every individual or group who might have an interest in the project.
2. **Analyzing the Project Charter**: Review the project charter or scope document, which may already identify key stakeholders or suggest additional parties based on project objectives and deliverables.
3. **Conducting Interviews**: Interview team members, department heads, or sponsors to gather input on who the key stakeholders might be.
4. **Using Stakeholder Registers from Similar Projects**: Examine stakeholder registers or lists from past or similar projects, as they may help identify individuals or groups relevant to the current project.

Typical Stakeholders in a Project:

- **Project Sponsor**: The person or group who funds the project.
- **Project Manager**: Responsible for leading the project.
- **Project Team**: Individuals working directly on the project's tasks.
- **Customers/Clients**: The recipients of the project's outcomes.
- **Vendors/Suppliers**: Those providing goods or services to the project.
- **Regulatory Bodies**: Organizations ensuring compliance with laws and regulations.
- **End Users**: People who will directly use the project's deliverables.

Step 2: Analyzing Stakeholders' Influence and Interest

Once stakeholders are identified, the next step is to analyze their level of influence and interest in the project. Understanding their power, needs, and expectations helps in prioritizing engagement strategies. This can be done using a **Stakeholder Analysis**.

A popular tool for stakeholder analysis is the **Stakeholder Influence/Interest Matrix**, which classifies stakeholders into four quadrants based on their influence over the project and their interest in its outcomes:

1. **High Influence, High Interest**: These stakeholders are critical to project success. They should be actively involved and kept fully informed, such as project sponsors or senior management.
2. **High Influence, Low Interest**: These stakeholders may not be deeply concerned with day-to-day project details but hold significant power. Keep them satisfied but do not overwhelm them with information, such as regulatory bodies or top-level executives.
3. **Low Influence, High Interest**: These stakeholders are very interested in the project but lack decision-making power. Keep them informed and engaged, as they can be advocates for the project. Examples include end users or team members.
4. **Low Influence, Low Interest**: These stakeholders have minimal involvement and power. They require minimal communication, but their needs should still be acknowledged.

This matrix helps in designing communication and engagement strategies tailored to each stakeholder group's influence and interest level.

Step 3: Developing a Stakeholder Engagement Plan

Engaging stakeholders effectively requires a well-structured plan. A **Stakeholder Engagement Plan** outlines how and when to communicate with each stakeholder or group, based on their needs, influence, and expectations.

Components of a Stakeholder Engagement Plan:

1. **Stakeholder Mapping**: Use the Stakeholder Influence/Interest Matrix to prioritize stakeholders based on their position in the matrix.
2. **Communication Methods**: Determine how each stakeholder will be communicated with, whether through formal reports, emails, meetings, or presentations. For example, high-interest stakeholders may require regular face-to-face meetings, while low-interest stakeholders might only need occasional updates.
3. **Frequency of Communication**: Define how often each stakeholder will receive updates. This could range from weekly status reports to monthly executive summaries.
4. **Key Messages**: Tailor your messages to address each stakeholder's concerns and expectations. For example, senior management might focus on financial metrics, while end users may be more interested in product functionality.
5. **Feedback Mechanism**: Include ways to gather feedback from stakeholders throughout the project. This could involve surveys, interviews, or informal discussions, allowing you to adjust the project based on their input.

Step 4: Engaging Stakeholders Throughout the Project Lifecycle

Stakeholder engagement is not a one-time activity; it must be ongoing throughout the project lifecycle.

Building strong relationships and maintaining open lines of communication are essential to gaining support and addressing concerns proactively.

Tips for Ongoing Stakeholder Engagement:

- **Active Listening**: Actively listen to stakeholders' concerns and feedback. This fosters trust and helps identify issues early.
- **Regular Updates**: Provide consistent, transparent updates on project progress, challenges, and changes. This ensures stakeholders are always aware of the project's status.
- **Managing Expectations**: Be realistic in your communication, and manage expectations by providing accurate timelines, budgets, and deliverable information. Avoid over-promising.
- **Conflict Resolution**: If conflicts arise, address them early. Conflicts may stem from misunderstandings, competing interests, or scope changes. Having a conflict resolution process in place ensures swift and fair resolutions.
- **Stakeholder Involvement in Key Decisions**: Involve stakeholders in major decisions, especially those that impact project scope, timeline, or deliverables. This not only secures their buy-in but also reduces resistance to changes.
- **Celebrate Successes**: Acknowledge and celebrate key milestones and successes with stakeholders. This reinforces their investment in the project and maintains positive relationships.

Challenges in Stakeholder Engagement

Engaging stakeholders effectively can be challenging, particularly when there are competing interests, conflicting priorities, or difficult personalities. Here are some common challenges and solutions:

1. **Conflicting Priorities**: Different stakeholders may have conflicting goals or demands. Address this by facilitating discussions and finding common ground, focusing on the overall success of the project.
2. **Lack of Engagement**: Some stakeholders may be disinterested or hard to engage. Use personalized communication methods that appeal to their interests and demonstrate the value they stand to gain from the project.
3. **Over-Engagement**: Overloading stakeholders with information or involving them in too many decisions can lead to frustration. Balance engagement levels by focusing on what matters most to each stakeholder.
4. **Changing Stakeholder Dynamics**: As the project progresses, new stakeholders may emerge, or existing ones may change in terms of influence or interest. Be adaptable and revisit your stakeholder engagement plan regularly.

Conclusion

Effective stakeholder identification and engagement are vital for the success of any project. By identifying stakeholders early, analyzing their influence and interests, and developing a tailored engagement plan, project managers can build strong relationships that foster collaboration and support.

Chapter 5: Team Building and Leadership

In project management, the success of a project heavily relies on the effectiveness of the project team and the leadership guiding it. Building a cohesive team and providing strong leadership are essential components that contribute to achieving project objectives and fostering a productive work environment. This chapter explores the principles of team building, effective leadership styles, and the strategies needed to create and maintain high-performing project teams.

Understanding Team Dynamics

A project team comprises individuals with diverse skills, experiences, and perspectives who come together to achieve a common goal. Understanding team dynamics is essential for building a successful team, as it influences collaboration, communication, and overall productivity. Key aspects of team dynamics include:

1. **Roles and Responsibilities**: Each team member should have a clear understanding of their role and responsibilities within the project. This clarity helps in reducing confusion and ensuring that all aspects of the project are covered.
2. **Interpersonal Relationships**: Building positive relationships among team members enhances

collaboration and fosters a supportive atmosphere. Trust, respect, and open communication are vital for creating a healthy team culture.

3. **Conflict Resolution**: Conflicts are inevitable in any team due to differing opinions, work styles, and personalities. Having effective conflict resolution strategies is crucial for maintaining harmony and ensuring that conflicts do not derail the project.

4. **Team Development Stages**: Teams typically progress through several stages of development, as outlined by Bruce Tuckman's model:

   o **Forming**: Team members get to know each other, define roles, and set initial goals.
   o **Storming**: Differences in opinions and working styles may lead to conflicts and power struggles.
   o **Norming**: The team begins to establish norms, build relationships, and find common ground.
   o **Performing**: The team operates at a high level of efficiency, collaborating effectively to achieve project goals.
   o **Adjourning**: The project concludes, and the team disbands, reflecting on the achievements and lessons learned.

Building a High-Performing Team

To create a high-performing team, project managers should focus on several key principles:

1. **Selecting the Right Team Members**: Choose team members based on their skills, experiences, and cultural fit. A diverse team with complementary skills enhances creativity and problem-solving capabilities.
2. **Defining Clear Goals**: Establish clear and measurable goals for the project. Communicate these goals to the team to ensure everyone is aligned and understands the desired outcomes.
3. **Fostering Open Communication**: Create an environment where team members feel comfortable expressing their ideas, concerns, and feedback. Regular check-ins and open-door policies encourage transparency and collaboration.
4. **Encouraging Collaboration**: Facilitate collaboration through team-building activities, brainstorming sessions, and joint problem-solving exercises. Encourage team members to share their expertise and support one another.
5. **Providing Resources and Support**: Ensure that the team has access to the necessary resources, tools, and training to succeed. This includes providing ongoing support and guidance to help team members overcome challenges.
6. **Recognizing and Rewarding Contributions**: Acknowledge individual and team accomplishments to boost morale and motivation. Celebrate milestones and successes,

and provide constructive feedback to encourage continuous improvement.

Leadership Styles in Project Management

Effective leadership is pivotal in guiding the project team toward success. Different leadership styles can be employed based on the project's needs, the team's dynamics, and individual team members' characteristics. Here are some common leadership styles:

1. **Transformational Leadership**: Transformational leaders inspire and motivate their teams by fostering a shared vision and encouraging personal and professional growth. They empower team members to take ownership of their roles and contribute creatively to the project.
2. **Transactional Leadership**: This style focuses on structure, rewards, and performance management. Transactional leaders establish clear expectations and provide feedback based on team members' performance. This approach is effective in environments that require strict adherence to processes and deadlines.
3. **Servant Leadership**: Servant leaders prioritize the needs of their team members, aiming to support and empower them. They actively listen, facilitate collaboration, and promote a culture of

trust and respect, ensuring that team members feel valued and engaged.

4. **Situational Leadership**: Situational leaders adapt their leadership style based on the team's maturity, the project's complexity, and the specific challenges being faced. They assess the situation and modify their approach accordingly, providing the right level of guidance and support.

5. **Democratic Leadership**: This style involves the team in decision-making processes, fostering a sense of ownership and collaboration. Democratic leaders encourage input from all team members, promoting a culture of shared responsibility.

Developing Leadership Skills

To lead a project team effectively, project managers should develop essential leadership skills, including:

1. **Effective Communication**: Clear and concise communication is vital for conveying expectations, providing feedback, and resolving conflicts. Developing active listening skills helps in understanding team members' concerns and needs.

2. **Emotional Intelligence**: Understanding and managing one's emotions, as well as empathizing with others, is key to building

strong relationships and maintaining a positive team culture. Leaders with high emotional intelligence can navigate team dynamics and motivate their members effectively.

3. **Decision-Making**: Project managers must be decisive and able to make informed decisions quickly. This includes analyzing data, considering stakeholders' perspectives, and weighing potential risks before making choices.

4. **Conflict Management**: Developing conflict resolution skills enables leaders to address issues promptly and constructively, minimizing disruptions and fostering a collaborative environment.

5. **Adaptability**: Projects often encounter unexpected changes and challenges. Being adaptable and open to new ideas allows leaders to pivot strategies and maintain team morale in the face of uncertainty.

6. **Mentoring and Coaching**: Supporting the development of team members through mentoring and coaching enhances their skills and confidence, contributing to overall team success.

Creating a Positive Team Culture

The culture within the project team significantly impacts performance and morale. Creating a positive team culture involves:

1. **Encouraging Diversity and Inclusion**: Embrace diverse perspectives and backgrounds within the team. An inclusive culture fosters creativity and innovation by encouraging team members to share unique ideas and experiences.
2. **Promoting Work-Life Balance**: Support team members in maintaining a healthy work-life balance by being mindful of workload and deadlines. Encourage breaks and flexibility to prevent burnout.
3. **Fostering Collaboration**: Create opportunities for collaboration and team bonding through team-building activities, workshops, and social events. These interactions strengthen relationships and enhance team cohesion.
4. **Encouraging Continuous Improvement**: Foster a culture of learning by encouraging team members to seek feedback, reflect on their performance, and pursue professional development opportunities.
5. **Instilling a Sense of Purpose**: Help team members understand the significance of their work within the broader context of the project and the organization. When team members see the impact of their contributions, it fosters motivation and engagement.

Conclusion

Effective team building and leadership are fundamental to project success. By fostering a cohesive team, employing suitable leadership styles, and creating a positive team culture, project managers can maximize their teams' potential and drive projects to successful completion.

Chapter 6: Project Scope Management

Project scope management is a critical aspect of project management that ensures the project delivers what it is intended to achieve while staying within defined boundaries. It involves defining, controlling, and monitoring what is included and excluded in the project. Proper scope management helps prevent scope creep, enhances stakeholder satisfaction, and ensures that resources are utilized efficiently. This chapter will explore the essential processes involved in project scope management and provide strategies for effective scope planning and execution.

Understanding Project Scope

Project scope refers to the sum of all deliverables, tasks, and requirements necessary to complete a project. It outlines what the project will achieve and delineates the boundaries of the project, including the work that needs to be performed as well as the work that is excluded.

Key Components of Project Scope:

- **Deliverables**: The specific outputs or products that the project is expected to produce.

- **Requirements**: The conditions or capabilities that must be met for the project deliverables to be accepted by stakeholders.
- **Exclusions**: Clearly defined aspects that are not included in the project, which helps to manage stakeholder expectations and avoid misunderstandings.

The Importance of Scope Management

Effective project scope management is essential for several reasons:

1. **Clarity**: Clearly defined project scope provides clarity to the project team and stakeholders, helping everyone understand what is expected and what will be delivered.
2. **Resource Management**: Proper scope management ensures that resources (time, budget, personnel) are allocated appropriately and used efficiently.
3. **Stakeholder Satisfaction**: By defining and managing scope, project managers can align expectations and deliverables with stakeholders, increasing satisfaction with the final outcomes.
4. **Minimizing Scope Creep**: Scope creep refers to uncontrolled changes or continuous growth in a project's scope. Effective scope management helps mitigate scope creep, which can lead to delays, budget overruns, and project failure.

Key Processes in Project Scope Management

Project scope management involves several key processes, as defined by the Project Management Institute (PMI):

1. **Scope Planning**
2. **Scope Definition**
3. **Create WBS (Work Breakdown Structure)**
4. **Scope Verification**
5. **Scope Control**

Let's explore each of these processes in detail.

1. Scope Planning

Scope planning involves developing a scope management plan that outlines how the project scope will be defined, validated, and controlled. This plan serves as a guide for managing scope throughout the project lifecycle.

Components of a Scope Management Plan:

- **Process for Scope Definition**: Describes how project scope will be defined, including techniques for gathering requirements.
- **Process for Scope Validation**: Outlines how deliverables will be verified and accepted by stakeholders.
- **Process for Scope Control**: Details how changes to the project scope will be managed and documented.

Techniques for Scope Planning:

- **Consulting Stakeholders**: Engaging with key stakeholders to gather their input on project goals and requirements.
- **Reviewing Organizational Standards**: Understanding company policies and standards that might affect project scope.

2. Scope Definition

Scope definition is the process of developing a detailed description of the project and its deliverables. It involves gathering requirements and translating them into clear objectives.

Steps for Effective Scope Definition:

- **Requirements Gathering**: Utilize techniques such as interviews, surveys, focus groups, and workshops to gather input from stakeholders about their needs and expectations.
- **Documenting Requirements**: Clearly document all requirements in a requirements management plan, ensuring they are measurable and testable.
- **Defining Project Boundaries**: Clearly articulate what is included in the project (in-scope) and what is excluded (out-of-scope). This helps set realistic expectations.

Tools for Scope Definition:

- **Requirements Traceability Matrix**: A tool used to track project requirements and ensure they are met throughout the project lifecycle.
- **User Stories and Use Cases**: Narrative descriptions that outline how users will interact with the system or product, helping to clarify requirements.

3. Create WBS (Work Breakdown Structure)

Creating a Work Breakdown Structure (WBS) is a critical step in project scope management. The WBS breaks down the project into smaller, manageable components, making it easier to define and manage tasks.

Steps to Create a WBS:

- **Identify Major Deliverables**: Begin by identifying the major deliverables of the project based on the scope definition.
- **Break Down Deliverables**: Decompose each major deliverable into smaller, more manageable tasks or work packages. Each work package should represent a unit of work that can be estimated, assigned, and tracked.
- **Develop WBS Dictionary**: Create a WBS dictionary that provides detailed descriptions of each element in the WBS, including deliverables, activities, and associated costs.

Benefits of a WBS:

- **Improved Clarity**: A WBS provides a clear visual representation of the project scope, making it easier for team members to understand their responsibilities.
- **Enhanced Estimation**: Breaking the project into smaller components allows for more accurate estimation of time and resources.

4. Scope Verification

Scope verification is the process of formalizing acceptance of the completed project deliverables. It ensures that the project has met the requirements outlined in the project scope.

Steps for Scope Verification:

- **Conduct Reviews**: Schedule formal reviews with stakeholders to evaluate the deliverables against the project scope and requirements.
- **Obtain Stakeholder Approval**: Secure sign-off from stakeholders to confirm that the deliverables meet their expectations.
- **Document Acceptance**: Record stakeholder acceptance and any feedback for future reference.

Importance of Scope Verification:

- **Ensures Alignment**: Regular verification helps ensure that the project remains aligned with stakeholder expectations.
- **Facilitates Change Management**: Documenting acceptance provides a baseline for managing any future changes to the scope.

5. Scope Control

Scope control involves monitoring the project scope and managing changes to prevent scope creep. It ensures that any changes are assessed, approved, and documented appropriately.

Steps for Effective Scope Control:

- **Monitor Scope Performance**: Regularly review project performance against the defined scope to identify any deviations or issues.
- **Implement Change Control Procedures**: Establish a formal process for requesting, evaluating, and approving changes to the project scope. This may include a Change Control Board (CCB) to evaluate requests.
- **Update Project Documentation**: Ensure that all changes to the project scope are documented and reflected in the project plans, including the WBS and requirements documentation.

Tips for Managing Scope Creep:

- **Communicate the Importance of Scope Management**: Educate stakeholders on the impact of scope creep and the importance of adhering to the defined scope.
- **Engage Stakeholders in Change Discussions**: Involve stakeholders in discussions about potential changes, helping them understand the implications on the project timeline and budget.

Conclusion

Effective project scope management is vital for delivering projects on time and within budget while meeting stakeholder expectations. By defining, verifying, and controlling the project scope, project managers can minimize risks, enhance collaboration, and ensure the successful completion of project objectives.

Chapter 7: Risk Management and Mitigation

In the dynamic landscape of project management, risk management plays a crucial role in ensuring project success. Every project is subject to uncertainties that can impact its timeline, budget, and overall outcomes. Effective risk management involves identifying, assessing, and responding to these risks proactively, minimizing their impact on the project. This chapter delves into the principles and practices of risk management, providing strategies for effective risk mitigation.

Understanding Risk Management

Risk in project management refers to any uncertain event or condition that, if it occurs, can affect the project's objectives—positively or negatively. Managing risks effectively is essential for safeguarding the project's success and achieving stakeholder satisfaction.

Key Components of Risk Management:

- **Risk Identification**: The process of determining potential risks that could affect the project.
- **Risk Assessment**: Analyzing and evaluating the identified risks to understand their potential impact and likelihood of occurrence.

- **Risk Response Planning**: Developing strategies to address identified risks, including mitigation, acceptance, transfer, or avoidance.
- **Risk Monitoring and Control**: Continuously tracking identified risks and evaluating the effectiveness of response strategies throughout the project lifecycle.

The Importance of Risk Management

Implementing a robust risk management process is crucial for several reasons:

1. **Enhances Decision-Making**: Understanding potential risks allows project managers to make informed decisions, prioritize tasks, and allocate resources effectively.
2. **Minimizes Uncertainties**: By identifying and addressing risks early, project managers can minimize uncertainties and avoid surprises that could derail the project.
3. **Protects Project Objectives**: Effective risk management safeguards project objectives, ensuring that projects are delivered on time, within budget, and to the satisfaction of stakeholders.
4. **Improves Stakeholder Confidence**: A proactive approach to risk management instills confidence in stakeholders, demonstrating that potential challenges are being addressed and managed.

The Risk Management Process

The risk management process consists of several key steps that guide project managers in effectively identifying and addressing risks:

1. Risk Identification

Risk identification involves systematically identifying potential risks that could impact the project. This process can be conducted using various techniques:

- **Brainstorming**: Involve team members and stakeholders in a brainstorming session to generate a list of potential risks based on their experiences and insights.
- **Interviews**: Conduct interviews with key stakeholders and subject matter experts to gather their perspectives on possible risks.
- **SWOT Analysis**: Analyze the project's Strengths, Weaknesses, Opportunities, and Threats (SWOT) to identify internal and external risks.
- **Historical Data Review**: Examine past projects to identify risks that have occurred previously, as well as lessons learned.
- **Checklists**: Utilize risk checklists based on industry standards and previous projects to ensure no significant risks are overlooked.

Documentation: As risks are identified, document them in a risk register, which serves as a central repository for all project risks.

2. Risk Assessment

Once risks have been identified, the next step is to assess their potential impact and likelihood of occurrence. This involves two main components:

- **Qualitative Risk Assessment**: Evaluate risks based on their probability of occurrence and potential impact on project objectives. This can be done using a risk matrix to categorize risks as low, medium, or high.
- **Quantitative Risk Assessment**: For critical risks, perform quantitative analysis to determine their potential financial impact or effect on project timelines. Techniques such as Monte Carlo simulations or decision tree analysis can be utilized to quantify risks.

Prioritization: Based on the assessment, prioritize risks to focus on those that pose the most significant threat to the project. High-priority risks should receive immediate attention and mitigation planning.

3. Risk Response Planning

After assessing the risks, the next step is to develop strategies for addressing them. Common risk response strategies include:

- **Risk Mitigation**: Taking proactive steps to reduce the probability or impact of a risk. This could involve implementing preventive measures, improving processes, or providing additional training.
- **Risk Acceptance**: Accepting the risk without taking any action, often appropriate for low-impact or low-probability risks. It's important to document the rationale for acceptance and to establish contingency plans.
- **Risk Transfer**: Shifting the risk to a third party, often through contracts or insurance. This strategy does not eliminate the risk but places the burden on another entity.
- **Risk Avoidance**: Altering project plans or objectives to eliminate the risk entirely. This may involve changing the project scope, timeline, or resource allocation.

Action Plans: Develop detailed action plans for each high-priority risk, outlining specific steps to be taken, responsible parties, and timelines.

4. Risk Monitoring and Control

Risk management is an ongoing process that requires continuous monitoring and control throughout the project lifecycle. This involves:

- **Regular Risk Reviews**: Schedule periodic reviews of the risk register to assess the status of identified risks, evaluate the effectiveness of response strategies, and identify new risks.
- **Tracking Risk Triggers**: Monitor key indicators or triggers that may signal the onset of a risk. Being vigilant about potential warning signs enables project managers to take timely action.
- **Adjusting Response Plans**: If a risk occurs or its status changes, adjust the response plans accordingly. Flexibility in response strategies is essential for effective risk management.
- **Communication**: Maintain open lines of communication with stakeholders regarding risks, responses, and any changes to the risk landscape.

Tools and Techniques for Risk Management

Several tools and techniques can aid in effective risk management:

- **Risk Register**: A central document that lists all identified risks, their assessments, response plans, and status updates. It serves as a valuable reference for the project team.
- **Risk Matrix**: A visual tool that categorizes risks based on their likelihood and impact, helping prioritize which risks require immediate attention.

- **SWOT Analysis**: An analytical tool that helps identify internal and external factors affecting the project, enabling a holistic view of risks.
- **Monte Carlo Simulation**: A quantitative analysis technique that uses statistical modeling to predict the probability of different outcomes based on identified risks.
- **Decision Trees**: A visual representation of decisions and their potential consequences, aiding in evaluating different risk response strategies.

Conclusion

Effective risk management and mitigation are critical to ensuring project success in an uncertain environment. By systematically identifying, assessing, and responding to risks, project managers can minimize their impact on project objectives, enhance stakeholder satisfaction, and improve overall project performance.

Chapter 8: Budgeting and Cost Management

Effective budgeting and cost management are vital components of successful project management. A well-defined budget not only ensures that resources are allocated efficiently but also helps in monitoring and controlling project costs throughout its lifecycle. This chapter will explore the principles of budgeting, techniques for cost estimation, and strategies for managing and controlling project costs.

Understanding Budgeting in Project Management

Budgeting in project management refers to the process of estimating the financial resources required to complete a project successfully. This involves forecasting costs for all project activities, creating a comprehensive budget, and monitoring expenses throughout the project's duration.

Key Components of Project Budgeting:

- **Cost Estimation**: The process of predicting the costs associated with project activities, including labor, materials, equipment, and overhead.
- **Budget Development**: Creating a formal budget document that outlines the total project cost and allocates funds to specific activities.

- **Cost Control**: Monitoring and managing project expenses to ensure that they stay within the approved budget.

The Importance of Budgeting and Cost Management

Implementing effective budgeting and cost management practices is essential for several reasons:

1. **Resource Allocation**: A well-prepared budget helps project managers allocate resources efficiently, ensuring that funds are available when needed.
2. **Financial Accountability**: Budgeting establishes a financial framework that holds project managers accountable for spending decisions and helps track financial performance.
3. **Risk Mitigation**: By identifying potential cost overruns early, effective budgeting allows project managers to take corrective action before problems escalate.
4. **Stakeholder Confidence**: A transparent budget fosters trust among stakeholders, demonstrating that the project is being managed responsibly and financially.

The Budgeting Process

The budgeting process involves several key steps that guide project managers in developing an accurate and comprehensive project budget:

1. Cost Estimation

Cost estimation is the first step in the budgeting process and involves predicting the costs associated with all project activities. There are several techniques for estimating costs:

- **Analogous Estimating**: Using historical data from similar projects to estimate costs. This method is quick and often relies on expert judgment but may not always be accurate due to differences between projects.
- **Parametric Estimating**: Utilizing statistical relationships between historical data and other variables (e.g., cost per square foot for construction projects) to estimate costs. This method can yield more accurate results if the parameters are well-defined.
- **Bottom-Up Estimating**: Breaking down the project into smaller components (work packages) and estimating costs for each component. These individual estimates are then aggregated to form the total project cost. This method is detailed and thorough but can be time-consuming.
- **Three-Point Estimating**: Involves estimating three values for each cost element: the most likely cost, the best-case cost (optimistic), and the worst-case cost (pessimistic). The final estimate is calculated using a weighted average. This technique accounts for uncertainty and risk.

Documentation: As costs are estimated, document them in a cost management plan that outlines the estimation methods used and any assumptions made during the process.

2. Budget Development

Once costs have been estimated, the next step is to develop the project budget. This involves consolidating all estimated costs into a formal budget document that outlines the total project cost and how funds will be allocated.

Components of a Project Budget:

- **Direct Costs**: Costs that can be directly attributed to project activities, such as labor, materials, and equipment.
- **Indirect Costs**: Costs that are not directly tied to specific project activities but are necessary for project execution, such as administrative expenses and utilities.
- **Contingency Reserves**: Additional funds set aside to address unforeseen circumstances or risks that may arise during the project.
- **Management Reserves**: Funds reserved for overall project management purposes, not assigned to specific tasks.

Creating a Budget Plan: Develop a budget plan that outlines how costs will be tracked, reported, and managed throughout the project. This plan should include:

- **Cost Baseline**: A reference point that includes all approved costs, used for measuring performance.
- **Budget Updates**: Guidelines for updating the budget as project conditions change or new information becomes available.

3. Cost Control

Cost control involves monitoring and managing project expenses to ensure that they stay within the approved budget. This includes tracking costs, comparing actual expenses to the budget, and taking corrective actions when necessary.

Techniques for Cost Control:

- **Performance Measurement**: Use tools such as Earned Value Management (EVM) to assess project performance against the baseline. EVM integrates cost, schedule, and scope to provide insights into project health.
- **Regular Budget Reviews**: Conduct periodic budget reviews to assess financial performance and identify variances. These reviews should involve comparing actual costs against the budgeted costs to determine any discrepancies.
- **Forecasting**: Regularly update forecasts to predict future expenses based on current project

performance. Adjust the budget as necessary to account for any changes or anticipated risks.

- **Change Control Process**: Implement a formal change control process to manage changes to the project scope or budget. This ensures that any alterations are documented, evaluated, and approved before being implemented.

Tools and Techniques for Budgeting and Cost Management

Several tools and techniques can aid project managers in budgeting and cost management:

- **Cost Management Plan**: A formal document that outlines how costs will be estimated, managed, and controlled throughout the project. It serves as a guide for the project team and stakeholders.
- **Budget Tracking Software**: Utilize project management software that includes budgeting features to monitor expenses, generate reports, and provide real-time insights into financial performance.
- **Variance Analysis**: A technique used to analyze the differences between budgeted and actual costs. This helps identify areas where performance deviates from the plan and allows for corrective actions to be taken.
- **Gantt Charts**: Visual representations of project timelines that can also be used to track

budgeted costs against scheduled activities. Gantt charts help visualize the relationship between time and cost.

Conclusion

Budgeting and cost management are essential for ensuring project success and achieving stakeholder satisfaction. By effectively estimating costs, developing comprehensive budgets, and controlling expenses throughout the project lifecycle, project managers can minimize risks, allocate resources efficiently, and enhance overall project performance.

Chapter 9: Time Management and Scheduling

Time management and scheduling are critical aspects of project management, influencing the overall success and timely completion of a project. Effective time management ensures that project tasks are completed as planned and that resources are utilized efficiently. This chapter explores the principles of time management, techniques for developing project schedules, and strategies for monitoring and controlling project timelines.

Understanding Time Management in Project Management

Time management in project management refers to the process of planning, estimating, and controlling the time required to complete a project. This involves setting a project timeline, defining milestones, and scheduling tasks to ensure that project objectives are met within the specified timeframe.

Key Components of Time Management:

- **Activity Definition**: Identifying and defining the specific tasks and activities required to complete the project.
- **Activity Sequencing**: Determining the order in which tasks should be performed, taking into account dependencies and relationships between tasks.

- **Duration Estimation**: Estimating the time required to complete each activity based on historical data, expert judgment, and team input.
- **Schedule Development**: Creating a project schedule that outlines when each activity will start and finish, along with milestones and deadlines.
- **Schedule Monitoring and Control**: Tracking progress against the schedule and making adjustments as needed to stay on track.

The Importance of Time Management

Implementing effective time management practices is essential for several reasons:

1. **Project Success**: Timely completion of project tasks is critical for achieving project objectives and delivering value to stakeholders.
2. **Resource Optimization**: Proper scheduling allows project managers to allocate resources efficiently, reducing downtime and maximizing productivity.
3. **Risk Mitigation**: By identifying potential scheduling conflicts and bottlenecks early, project managers can take corrective actions to minimize delays and disruptions.
4. **Stakeholder Satisfaction**: Meeting project deadlines enhances stakeholder confidence and satisfaction, fostering trust and support for future projects.

The Time Management Process

The time management process consists of several key steps that guide project managers in effectively managing project schedules:

1. Activity Definition

The first step in time management is to define all the activities required to complete the project. This involves breaking down the project into smaller, manageable components. Techniques for activity definition include:

- **Work Breakdown Structure (WBS)**: A hierarchical decomposition of the project into smaller work packages. The WBS helps in identifying all the tasks necessary for project completion and organizes them logically.
- **Brainstorming Sessions**: Engage team members and stakeholders in brainstorming sessions to identify all activities associated with project deliverables.
- **Expert Judgment**: Leverage the experience and insights of project team members or subject matter experts to ensure all activities are identified.

2. Activity Sequencing

Once activities have been defined, the next step is to determine their sequence and dependencies. This involves understanding the relationships between tasks, which can be categorized as:

- **Finish-to-Start (FS)**: The most common relationship, where one task must finish before the next can start.
- **Start-to-Start (SS)**: Two tasks that can start simultaneously; one task must begin before the other can start.
- **Finish-to-Finish (FF)**: Two tasks that must finish simultaneously; one task must finish before the other can finish.
- **Start-to-Finish (SF)**: A less common relationship where one task must start before another can finish.

Tools for Sequencing: Utilize tools like dependency diagrams or precedence diagrams to visually represent task relationships and dependencies.

3. Duration Estimation

After sequencing activities, the next step is to estimate the duration required for each task. Techniques for duration estimation include:

- **Expert Judgment**: Consult experienced team members or subject matter experts to estimate how long tasks will take based on their knowledge and experience.

- **Historical Data**: Review data from previous projects to inform estimates, identifying trends or common durations for similar tasks.
- **Parametric Estimating**: Use statistical relationships to estimate durations. For example, if a similar task took ten days to complete, you might estimate that the new task will take a similar amount of time based on its size and complexity.
- **Three-Point Estimation**: As discussed in Chapter 8, this method involves estimating optimistic, pessimistic, and most likely durations to arrive at a weighted average.

4. Schedule Development

With defined activities, established sequences, and estimated durations, the next step is to develop the project schedule. This involves:

- **Creating a Gantt Chart**: A visual representation of the project schedule, displaying tasks along a timeline. Gantt charts help visualize start and end dates, task durations, and dependencies.
- **Critical Path Method (CPM)**: Identify the longest sequence of dependent tasks that determine the project's minimum duration. The critical path

highlights tasks that cannot be delayed without affecting the project's end date.

- **Program Evaluation and Review Technique (PERT)**: A statistical tool used to analyze the time required to complete each task and assess the impact of uncertainty on the project schedule.
- **Milestones**: Establish significant points in the project timeline to measure progress and achievements. Milestones help stakeholders track project status and maintain momentum.

5. Schedule Monitoring and Control

Once the schedule is established, continuous monitoring and control are necessary to ensure that the project stays on track. Techniques for effective schedule control include:

- **Regular Status Meetings**: Conduct periodic meetings to review progress, discuss challenges, and ensure that the project remains aligned with the schedule.
- **Progress Tracking**: Use project management software to track the completion of tasks against the established schedule. This allows for real-time updates and visibility into project status.
- **Variance Analysis**: Assess deviations from the schedule, identifying any tasks that are ahead of or behind schedule. Analyze the causes of variances and take corrective actions as needed.

- **Revising the Schedule**: If significant delays occur or changes arise, be prepared to revise the schedule. Adjust resource allocations, re-sequence tasks, or change deadlines as necessary to maintain project momentum.

Tools and Techniques for Time Management and Scheduling

Several tools and techniques can aid project managers in effective time management and scheduling:

- **Gantt Chart Software**: Utilize project management software that includes Gantt chart features to create, manage, and visualize project timelines.
- **Critical Path Analysis Tools**: Leverage tools designed for critical path analysis to identify dependencies and optimize scheduling.
- **Project Management Software**: Use comprehensive project management tools that allow for planning, tracking, and collaboration, facilitating effective communication among team members.
- **Time Tracking Tools**: Implement time tracking tools to monitor time spent on tasks, allowing for accurate reporting and assessment of team productivity.

Conclusion

Effective time management and scheduling are essential for ensuring project success and achieving stakeholder satisfaction. By systematically defining activities, sequencing tasks, estimating durations, and monitoring progress, project managers can optimize resource utilization, mitigate risks, and deliver projects on time.

Chapter 10: Communication Planning and Execution

Effective communication is a cornerstone of successful project management. A well-structured communication plan ensures that all stakeholders are informed, engaged, and aligned with project goals. This chapter delves into the principles of communication planning, strategies for executing communication plans, and techniques for fostering a culture of open and effective communication throughout the project lifecycle.

Understanding Communication in Project Management

Communication in project management refers to the processes through which information is exchanged among project stakeholders, including team members, clients, sponsors, and other interested parties. Effective communication facilitates collaboration, minimizes misunderstandings, and ensures that everyone is on the same page regarding project objectives, progress, and challenges.

Key Components of Communication Planning:

- **Identifying Stakeholders**: Understanding who needs information and their specific information requirements.

- **Defining Communication Objectives**: Establishing clear goals for what the communication should achieve.
- **Selecting Communication Channels**: Determining the most effective channels for delivering information (e.g., emails, meetings, reports).
- **Creating a Communication Schedule**: Developing a timeline for when and how often communication will occur.
- **Establishing Feedback Mechanisms**: Implementing processes for gathering feedback to improve communication effectiveness.

The Importance of Communication Planning

Implementing effective communication planning is essential for several reasons:

1. **Stakeholder Engagement**: Clear communication fosters stakeholder engagement, ensuring that everyone is informed about project developments and has a voice in the decision-making process.
2. **Minimizing Misunderstandings**: A structured communication plan reduces the likelihood of misunderstandings and misinterpretations, which can lead to project delays and conflicts.
3. **Building Trust**: Transparent and timely communication helps build trust among stakeholders, enhancing relationships and collaboration.
4. **Change Management**: Effective communication is crucial for managing change, as it helps stakeholders

understand the rationale behind decisions and the impact of changes on the project.

The Communication Planning Process

The communication planning process involves several key steps that guide project managers in developing an effective communication plan:

1. Identifying Stakeholders

The first step in communication planning is identifying all stakeholders involved in the project. This includes anyone who will be affected by the project or who has an interest in its outcome.

Stakeholder Identification Techniques:

- **Stakeholder Analysis**: Conduct a stakeholder analysis to assess their influence, interest, and communication needs. This helps prioritize communication efforts based on stakeholder importance.
- **Stakeholder Register**: Create a stakeholder register that documents key stakeholders, their roles, communication preferences, and contact information.

2. Defining Communication Objectives

Once stakeholders are identified, the next step is to define clear communication objectives. These objectives should align with overall project goals and specify what the communication aims to achieve.

Example Communication Objectives:

- Inform stakeholders of project progress and updates.
- Engage team members in decision-making processes.
- Gather feedback on project deliverables.
- Address concerns and manage expectations.

3. Selecting Communication Channels

Choosing the right communication channels is crucial for effective information exchange. Different stakeholders may prefer different channels, so it's important to consider their preferences and the nature of the information being communicated.

Common Communication Channels:

- **Email**: Suitable for formal communication, updates, and documentation.
- **Meetings**: Useful for discussions, brainstorming sessions, and decision-making.
- **Reports**: Effective for summarizing project progress and performance.

- **Instant Messaging**: Useful for quick updates and informal communication.
- **Project Management Software**: Centralized platforms that facilitate collaboration and information sharing among team members.

4. Creating a Communication Schedule

Developing a communication schedule outlines when and how often communication will occur. This schedule should align with project milestones and activities.

Components of a Communication Schedule:

- **Frequency**: Determine how often updates will be provided (e.g., weekly, bi-weekly, monthly).
- **Timing**: Schedule communication activities around key project phases or milestones.
- **Format**: Specify the format for communication (e.g., written reports, verbal updates) and who will be responsible for each communication activity.

5. Establishing Feedback Mechanisms

Implementing feedback mechanisms is essential for assessing the effectiveness of communication efforts and making necessary adjustments. This encourages a culture of open communication where stakeholders feel valued and heard.

Feedback Mechanisms:

- **Surveys and Questionnaires**: Collect feedback from stakeholders on the clarity and effectiveness of communication.
- **One-on-One Meetings**: Schedule individual meetings with key stakeholders to gather insights and address concerns.
- **Regular Check-ins**: Incorporate feedback discussions into regular project meetings to encourage ongoing dialogue.

Executing the Communication Plan

Once the communication plan is developed, effective execution is key to ensuring that information is disseminated appropriately and in a timely manner. Strategies for executing the communication plan include:

1. Clear and Concise Messaging

Ensure that all communication is clear, concise, and tailored to the audience. Use simple language and avoid jargon when communicating with stakeholders who may not be familiar with technical terms.

2. Consistent Updates

Regularly provide updates on project progress, milestones achieved, and any changes to the project scope or timeline. Consistency helps build trust and keeps stakeholders informed.

3. Engaging Stakeholders

Encourage stakeholder engagement by providing opportunities for feedback and input. Create forums for discussion, such as workshops or focus groups, to involve stakeholders in the decision-making process.

4. Monitoring Communication Effectiveness

Continuously assess the effectiveness of communication efforts by tracking stakeholder responses and engagement levels. Adjust communication strategies as necessary to enhance clarity and responsiveness.

5. Addressing Challenges

Be proactive in addressing communication challenges, such as language barriers, time zone differences, or conflicting priorities. Utilize translation services, schedule meetings at convenient times, and prioritize urgent communication to overcome these challenges.

Tools and Techniques for Communication Planning and Execution

Several tools and techniques can aid project managers in effective communication planning and execution:

- **Communication Management Plan**: Develop a formal document that outlines the communication strategy, including objectives, channels, schedule, and feedback mechanisms.
- **Collaboration Tools**: Utilize collaboration platforms such as Slack, Microsoft Teams, or Asana to facilitate communication among team members and streamline information sharing.
- **Meeting Agendas and Minutes**: Use structured meeting agendas to guide discussions and capture key points in meeting minutes to ensure that action items are documented and communicated.
- **Project Dashboards**: Implement project dashboards that provide real-time updates on project status, milestones, and key performance indicators, keeping stakeholders informed at all times.

Conclusion

Effective communication planning and execution are essential for fostering collaboration, minimizing misunderstandings, and ensuring project success. By systematically identifying stakeholders, defining communication objectives, selecting appropriate channels, and establishing feedback mechanisms, project managers can enhance engagement and build trust among stakeholders.

Chapter 11: Change Management in Projects

Change is an inevitable aspect of project management. As projects evolve, they may face various internal and external changes that can affect scope, timelines, resources, and overall objectives. Effective change management ensures that these changes are handled in a structured and systematic manner, minimizing disruption and maintaining project alignment with stakeholder expectations. This chapter explores the principles of change management, strategies for implementing change, and techniques for overcoming resistance to change.

Understanding Change Management in Project Management

Change management refers to the process of managing changes to a project's scope, goals, or resources in a way that minimizes disruption while maximizing stakeholder engagement and project success. It involves assessing, planning, implementing, and monitoring changes to ensure they align with project objectives and stakeholder needs.

Key Components of Change Management:

- **Change Identification**: Recognizing the need for change and documenting the details of the proposed change.
- **Change Assessment**: Analyzing the potential impacts of the change on the project scope, timeline, resources, and stakeholder expectations.
- **Change Approval**: Seeking formal approval from stakeholders or governing bodies before implementing changes.
- **Change Implementation**: Executing the approved changes while ensuring proper communication and engagement with all stakeholders.
- **Change Review**: Monitoring the implementation of changes to assess their effectiveness and make necessary adjustments.

The Importance of Change Management

Implementing effective change management practices is essential for several reasons:

1. **Minimizing Disruption**: Structured change management helps to minimize disruptions to project activities, ensuring that the project remains on track despite changes.
2. **Enhancing Stakeholder Engagement**: Involving stakeholders in the change process fosters collaboration and ensures that their concerns are addressed.
3. **Improving Project Outcomes**: Effective change management can lead to better project outcomes by

ensuring that changes are aligned with strategic objectives and stakeholder needs.

4. **Managing Risks**: By proactively identifying and managing changes, project managers can mitigate risks associated with unexpected developments.

The Change Management Process

The change management process consists of several key steps that guide project managers in effectively managing changes:

1. Change Identification

The first step in change management is to identify the need for change. Changes can arise from various sources, including:

- **Stakeholder Requests**: Stakeholders may request changes based on new information, shifting priorities, or evolving needs.
- **External Factors**: Changes in regulations, market conditions, or technology can necessitate adjustments to the project.
- **Project Performance**: Performance metrics may indicate the need for changes to improve efficiency or outcomes.

Documentation: Once a change is identified, it should be documented clearly, including the reason for the change, the proposed modifications, and any relevant supporting information.

2. Change Assessment

After a change has been identified, it is crucial to assess its potential impact on the project. This involves evaluating:

- **Scope**: How will the change affect the project scope? Will new deliverables be added, or existing deliverables be modified?
- **Timeline**: What is the anticipated impact on the project schedule? Will the change require additional time to implement?
- **Resources**: Will the change require additional resources (e.g., personnel, budget, materials) or affect existing resource allocations?
- **Stakeholder Expectations**: How will the change affect stakeholder expectations and project outcomes?

Impact Analysis: Conducting a thorough impact analysis helps project managers understand the implications of the change and informs decision-making.

3. Change Approval

Once the change has been assessed, the next step is to seek formal approval before implementation. This often involves presenting the proposed change to a change control board (CCB) or relevant stakeholders for review.

Approval Process:

- **Documentation**: Prepare a change request document outlining the details of the change, the rationale for the change, and the results of the impact analysis.
- **Review**: Present the change request to the appropriate stakeholders or governing body for review.
- **Decision**: Obtain formal approval or rejection of the change. If approved, determine any additional steps or conditions for implementation.

4. Change Implementation

After receiving approval, the change can be implemented. This step involves executing the necessary modifications while ensuring proper communication and engagement with stakeholders.

Implementation Strategies:

- **Communication Plan**: Develop a communication plan to inform stakeholders about the change, its rationale, and its anticipated impact on the project.
- **Training and Support**: Provide training and support to team members or stakeholders affected by the change, ensuring they understand the new processes or expectations.
- **Monitoring**: Monitor the implementation process to ensure that the change is executed as planned and that any issues are addressed promptly.

5. Change Review

Following implementation, it is essential to review the change to assess its effectiveness and make any necessary adjustments. This involves:

- **Performance Metrics**: Evaluate project performance against established metrics to determine whether the change has achieved its intended outcomes.
- **Stakeholder Feedback**: Gather feedback from stakeholders regarding their perceptions of the change and its impact on the project.
- **Continuous Improvement**: Use the insights gained from the review process to inform future change management efforts and improve overall project performance.

Overcoming Resistance to Change

Resistance to change is a common challenge in project management. Addressing resistance effectively is crucial for successful change implementation. Strategies for overcoming resistance include:

1. Involving Stakeholders

Engaging stakeholders early in the change process fosters a sense of ownership and encourages collaboration. Solicit input and feedback from stakeholders during the change assessment and approval phases.

2. Communicating Clearly

Provide clear and transparent communication about the change, its rationale, and its benefits. Address any concerns or misconceptions stakeholders may have to build trust and confidence in the change process.

3. Providing Support

Offer support and resources to help stakeholders adapt to the change. This may include training sessions, one-on-one coaching, or access to additional resources.

4. Demonstrating Benefits

Highlight the benefits of the change for both the project and stakeholders. Demonstrating how the change aligns with project goals and enhances outcomes can help mitigate resistance.

5. Being Flexible

Be open to feedback and willing to adjust the change implementation process as needed. Flexibility shows stakeholders that their concerns are valued and can lead to more successful outcomes.

Tools and Techniques for Change Management

Several tools and techniques can aid project managers in effective change management:

- **Change Control Systems**: Implement a formal change control system to document and track change requests, approvals, and implementation progress.
- **Stakeholder Analysis Tools**: Use stakeholder analysis tools to assess stakeholder interests and influence, helping to identify potential sources of resistance.
- **Communication Tools**: Utilize project management and communication tools (e.g., Slack, Microsoft Teams) to facilitate discussions and share updates related to changes.
- **Training and Development Programs**: Invest in training programs that help team members adapt to changes, enhancing their skills and knowledge related to new processes or technologies.

Conclusion

Effective change management is essential for navigating the complexities of project dynamics and ensuring project success. By systematically identifying, assessing, approving, implementing, and reviewing changes, project managers can minimize disruption, engage stakeholders, and align changes with project objectives.

Chapter 12: Resource Allocation and Management

Effective resource allocation and management are critical components of successful project management. Resources, including personnel, equipment, materials, and finances, must be efficiently allocated to ensure that project objectives are met on time and within budget. This chapter explores the principles of resource allocation, strategies for effective resource management, and techniques for optimizing resource utilization throughout the project lifecycle.

Understanding Resource Allocation and Management

Resource allocation refers to the process of assigning available resources to various tasks or project components in a way that maximizes efficiency and effectiveness. Proper resource management ensures that the right resources are available at the right time and place, enabling project teams to execute their tasks smoothly.

Key Components of Resource Management:

- **Identifying Resources**: Determining the types and quantities of resources needed for the project.
- **Resource Planning**: Developing a plan for how resources will be allocated and managed throughout the project lifecycle.

- **Resource Scheduling**: Establishing timelines for resource allocation and utilization based on project tasks and milestones.
- **Monitoring Resource Use**: Tracking resource consumption and performance to ensure alignment with project goals and objectives.

The Importance of Resource Allocation and Management

Implementing effective resource allocation and management practices is essential for several reasons:

1. **Optimal Resource Utilization**: Efficient allocation ensures that resources are used to their fullest potential, minimizing waste and reducing costs.
2. **Meeting Project Deadlines**: Proper resource management enables teams to meet deadlines by ensuring that the necessary resources are available when needed.
3. **Enhancing Team Performance**: Allocating the right resources to the right tasks fosters a productive work environment, boosting team morale and performance.
4. **Risk Mitigation**: Effective resource management helps identify potential resource constraints or bottlenecks, allowing project managers to address issues proactively.

The Resource Allocation Process

The resource allocation process consists of several key steps that guide project managers in effectively managing project resources:

1. Identifying Resources

The first step in resource allocation is to identify the resources required for the project. This includes personnel, equipment, materials, and financial resources.

Resource Identification Techniques:

- **Work Breakdown Structure (WBS)**: Develop a WBS to break down project deliverables into manageable tasks. This helps identify specific resources needed for each task.
- **Resource Matrix**: Create a resource matrix that outlines the resources required for each task, including skills, equipment, and materials.

2. Resource Planning

Once the necessary resources have been identified, the next step is to develop a resource management plan. This plan outlines how resources will be allocated and managed throughout the project lifecycle.

Key Elements of a Resource Management Plan:

- **Resource Availability**: Assess the availability of required resources, including personnel schedules, equipment availability, and material lead times.
- **Resource Constraints**: Identify any potential constraints that could impact resource allocation, such as budget limitations or competing priorities.
- **Resource Allocation Strategy**: Develop a strategy for allocating resources to tasks based on priority, resource availability, and project timelines.

3. Resource Scheduling

Establishing a resource schedule involves determining when and how resources will be allocated to specific tasks. This schedule should align with the overall project timeline and milestones.

Scheduling Techniques:

- **Gantt Charts**: Use Gantt charts to visually represent the timeline for resource allocation, showing which resources are assigned to which tasks and when.
- **Resource Leveling**: Implement resource leveling techniques to adjust the allocation of resources to ensure that they are utilized efficiently without overloading team members or causing delays.

4. Monitoring Resource Use

Once resources have been allocated and scheduled, it is essential to monitor their utilization throughout the project. This involves tracking resource consumption, performance, and any deviations from the plan.

Monitoring Techniques:

- **Key Performance Indicators (KPIs)**: Establish KPIs to assess resource utilization, such as hours worked, budget spent, and task completion rates.
- **Regular Check-Ins**: Conduct regular check-ins with team members to assess resource availability and address any issues that may arise.
- **Resource Utilization Reports**: Generate reports that provide insights into resource usage, helping identify trends, bottlenecks, or areas for improvement.

Strategies for Effective Resource Management

To enhance resource allocation and management, project managers can implement several strategies:

1. Prioritize Tasks

Identify critical tasks that require immediate attention and allocate resources accordingly. This ensures that the most important aspects of the project receive the necessary focus and support.

2. Foster Collaboration

Encourage collaboration among team members to share resources and knowledge effectively. Creating an environment that promotes teamwork enhances resource efficiency and problem-solving capabilities.

3. Utilize Technology

Leverage project management tools and software to streamline resource allocation and management processes. Tools like Microsoft Project, Trello, or Asana can help track resource availability, schedules, and performance metrics.

4. Build a Resource Pool

Develop a resource pool that includes a diverse range of skills and expertise within the team. This flexibility allows for easier reallocation of resources as project needs evolve.

5. Plan for Contingencies

Anticipate potential resource constraints or disruptions by developing contingency plans. This proactive approach ensures that the project can adapt to unforeseen circumstances without significant delays.

Challenges in Resource Allocation and Management

Despite best efforts, project managers may encounter various challenges in resource allocation and management:

1. Resource Conflicts

Competing priorities and demands for resources can lead to conflicts. To address this, prioritize tasks based on project goals and engage stakeholders in discussions about resource allocation.

2. Limited Resources

Constraints on budget, personnel, or equipment can impact resource availability. In such cases, consider reallocating resources from lower-priority tasks or seeking additional funding or support.

3. Unforeseen Changes

Changes in project scope, timelines, or external factors can disrupt resource plans. Maintain flexibility in resource allocation and be prepared to adapt as needed.

4. Team Dynamics

Poor team dynamics or conflicts among team members can hinder resource management efforts. Foster a positive team culture through open communication and collaboration.

Tools and Techniques for Resource Management

Several tools and techniques can aid project managers in effective resource management:

- **Resource Management Software**: Implement software solutions designed for resource management, such as Smartsheet or Resource Guru, to track resource allocation and utilization in real time.
- **Resource Allocation Matrices**: Utilize matrices to map resources to tasks, clearly identifying who is responsible for each deliverable and when they are needed.
- **Project Dashboards**: Create project dashboards that provide an overview of resource utilization, highlighting key metrics and areas for improvement.
- **Scenario Planning**: Use scenario planning techniques to assess the impact of potential changes in resource availability or project scope, helping to inform decision-making.

Conclusion

Effective resource allocation and management are essential for the success of any project. By systematically identifying, planning, scheduling, and monitoring resources, project managers can optimize resource utilization, enhance team performance, and ensure that project objectives are met on time and within budget.

Chapter 13: Agile vs. Waterfall: Choosing the Right Approach

In the realm of project management, selecting the appropriate methodology is crucial for achieving project success. Two of the most commonly used methodologies are Agile and Waterfall. Each has its strengths and weaknesses, making them suitable for different types of projects and organizational needs. This chapter delves into the key differences between Agile and Waterfall methodologies, their respective advantages and disadvantages, and guidance on how to choose the right approach for your project.

Understanding Agile and Waterfall Methodologies

Waterfall is a traditional project management approach characterized by a linear, sequential process. It consists of distinct phases, including requirements gathering, design, development, testing, and deployment. Each phase must be completed before moving on to the next, making it a rigid and structured methodology.

Agile, on the other hand, is an iterative and flexible approach that emphasizes collaboration, customer feedback, and rapid delivery of small, functional increments. Agile methodologies, such as Scrum and Kanban, allow teams to adapt to changing requirements and focus on delivering value continuously.

Key Differences Between Agile and Waterfall

1. **Project Structure**:
    - **Waterfall**: Follows a linear path, moving through predefined phases in a strict order. Each phase must be completed before the next begins, creating a clear project timeline.
    - **Agile**: Employs an iterative approach, allowing for cycles of planning, execution, and review. Teams can revisit and revise previous phases based on feedback and new information.

2. **Flexibility**:
    - **Waterfall**: Less flexible, as changes to requirements or scope can lead to significant disruptions. Any alterations typically require revisiting earlier phases, which can delay timelines and increase costs.
    - **Agile**: Highly flexible, enabling teams to respond quickly to changes in requirements, stakeholder feedback, or market conditions. Iterations allow for continuous improvement and adaptation.

3. **Customer Involvement**:
    - **Waterfall**: Customer involvement is primarily concentrated at the beginning (requirements gathering) and end (acceptance testing) of the project. This limited interaction can result in misalignment with customer expectations.
    - **Agile**: Involves customers and stakeholders throughout the project lifecycle. Continuous feedback is encouraged, ensuring that the

final product aligns closely with customer needs.

4. **Delivery**:
    o **Waterfall**: The final product is delivered only at the end of the project after all phases are completed. This can lead to longer wait times for stakeholders to see results.
    o **Agile**: Delivers functional increments of the product at regular intervals (sprints). This allows stakeholders to see progress and provides opportunities for early feedback.

5. **Risk Management**:
    o **Waterfall**: Risk management is typically addressed during the planning phase, with potential issues identified in advance. However, risks that emerge later in the process may be harder to address.
    o **Agile**: Emphasizes continuous risk assessment and mitigation throughout the project. Teams can identify and address risks as they arise, reducing the likelihood of major issues.

Advantages of Waterfall Methodology

- **Clarity and Structure**: Waterfall provides a clear and structured approach, making it easy to understand project phases and timelines.
- **Well-Defined Requirements**: It is suitable for projects with well-defined requirements and minimal expected changes, such as construction or manufacturing projects.

- **Comprehensive Documentation**: Waterfall often emphasizes detailed documentation, which can be beneficial for complex projects that require regulatory compliance or future reference.

Disadvantages of Waterfall Methodology

- **Inflexibility**: The rigid structure makes it challenging to accommodate changes in requirements or scope once the project is underway.
- **Late Feedback**: Limited customer involvement can lead to misalignment with stakeholder expectations, as feedback is often received only at the end of the project.
- **Risk of Failure**: If any phase fails, it can have a cascading effect on subsequent phases, potentially jeopardizing the entire project.

Advantages of Agile Methodology

- **Flexibility and Adaptability**: Agile allows teams to respond quickly to changes in requirements, stakeholder feedback, or market dynamics.
- **Continuous Improvement**: Iterative cycles promote continuous learning and improvement, enabling teams to refine their processes and deliverables.
- **Enhanced Customer Collaboration**: Regular customer involvement ensures that the final product aligns closely with stakeholder expectations and needs.

Disadvantages of Agile Methodology

- **Less Predictability**: The iterative nature of Agile can make it challenging to predict timelines and budgets accurately, as requirements may evolve throughout the project.
- **Potential for Scope Creep**: Without careful management, the flexibility of Agile can lead to scope creep, where additional requirements continuously emerge, jeopardizing project timelines.
- **Requires a Cultural Shift**: Implementing Agile methodologies may require a cultural shift within organizations, emphasizing collaboration and adaptability, which can be challenging to achieve.

Choosing the Right Approach

Selecting between Agile and Waterfall depends on several factors, including project type, organizational culture, and stakeholder needs. Here are some considerations to help guide the decision:

1. Nature of the Project

- **Waterfall**: Ideal for projects with clear, well-defined requirements and minimal expected changes, such as construction, manufacturing, or regulatory projects.
- **Agile**: Suitable for projects that are dynamic, with evolving requirements and a need for continuous feedback, such as software development, product design, or marketing campaigns.

2. Stakeholder Involvement

- **Waterfall**: Appropriate for projects where stakeholder involvement is limited to specific phases, such as initial requirements gathering and final testing.
- **Agile**: Best for projects where stakeholders are engaged throughout the process, providing continuous feedback and input.

3. Risk Tolerance

- **Waterfall**: Suitable for organizations with a low tolerance for risk and a preference for structured, predictable outcomes.
- **Agile**: Ideal for organizations willing to embrace uncertainty and adapt to changing circumstances.

4. Organizational Culture

- **Waterfall**: Often aligns with traditional organizational cultures that prioritize hierarchy and clear processes.
- **Agile**: Fits well within collaborative, adaptive organizational cultures that value teamwork and innovation.

5. Resource Availability

- **Waterfall**: May require a stable team with clearly defined roles and responsibilities.

- **Agile**: Benefits from cross-functional teams that can collaborate and adapt to changing demands.

Conclusion

Choosing between Agile and Waterfall methodologies requires careful consideration of project requirements, stakeholder needs, and organizational culture. Both methodologies offer distinct advantages and challenges, and understanding these can help project managers make informed decisions that align with project goals and objectives.

Chapter 14: Project Monitoring and Control

Effective project monitoring and control are essential components of successful project management. They ensure that projects remain on track, meet their objectives, and adhere to their budget and schedule. This chapter delves into the principles and practices of project monitoring and control, the tools and techniques used, and the importance of proactive management throughout the project lifecycle.

Understanding Project Monitoring and Control

Project Monitoring involves the continuous observation and assessment of project performance against established objectives. It allows project managers to track progress, identify deviations from the plan, and gather data necessary for informed decision-making.

Project Control, on the other hand, refers to the process of taking corrective actions to address any deviations from the project plan. It involves analyzing performance data, identifying variances, and implementing strategies to bring the project back on track.

The Importance of Monitoring and Control

Monitoring and control play a vital role in project success for several reasons:

1. **Performance Assessment**: Regular monitoring provides insights into how well the project is progressing compared to established metrics, enabling project managers to assess performance continuously.
2. **Early Detection of Issues**: Continuous monitoring allows for the early identification of potential problems or risks, enabling proactive measures to mitigate their impact.
3. **Resource Optimization**: Monitoring resource utilization helps identify areas where resources are being under or over-utilized, leading to better allocation and efficiency.
4. **Stakeholder Communication**: Regular updates and reports keep stakeholders informed of project status, fostering transparency and trust.

Key Components of Project Monitoring and Control

1. **Performance Measurement**: Establishing key performance indicators (KPIs) is essential for measuring project performance. KPIs should be aligned with project objectives and provide quantifiable metrics for tracking progress.
   o **Common KPIs:**

- Schedule Variance (SV): Measures the difference between the planned progress and actual progress.
- Cost Variance (CV): Compares the budgeted cost of work performed to the actual cost.
- Return on Investment (ROI): Evaluates the financial return from the project relative to its cost.

2. **Data Collection**: Gathering data from various sources is crucial for effective monitoring. This may involve tracking progress reports, financial data, resource utilization, and stakeholder feedback.

3. **Performance Analysis**: Analyzing performance data helps identify trends, variances, and potential issues. This analysis can involve:
   - **Variance Analysis**: Comparing planned versus actual performance to identify discrepancies.
   - **Trend Analysis**: Assessing performance over time to identify patterns and potential future performance.

4. **Reporting**: Regular reporting is essential for keeping stakeholders informed. This may include:
   - **Status Reports**: Providing updates on project progress, risks, and any issues encountered.
   - **Dashboards**: Using visual representations of key metrics for quick insights into project health.

5. **Risk Management**: Continuous monitoring allows project managers to identify new risks

and reassess existing ones. Regularly updating the risk management plan ensures that mitigation strategies remain effective.

6. **Change Management**: Projects often encounter changes in scope, resources, or timelines. A structured change management process allows project managers to assess the impact of changes and implement them systematically.

Tools and Techniques for Monitoring and Control

1. **Project Management Software**: Tools like Microsoft Project, Asana, or Trello provide functionalities for tracking tasks, timelines, and resources. These platforms often offer reporting features to visualize project performance.

2. **Earned Value Management (EVM)**: EVM is a powerful technique for measuring project performance and progress. It integrates scope, schedule, and cost data, allowing project managers to assess project health holistically.
   - **Key EVM Metrics**:
     - Planned Value (PV): The value of the work that was planned to be completed by a specific time.
     - Earned Value (EV): The value of the work that has actually been completed by that time.
     - Actual Cost (AC): The actual cost incurred for the work completed.

3. **Gantt Charts**: Gantt charts visually represent project timelines, showing task durations, dependencies, and progress. They are useful for tracking schedules and identifying delays.
4. **Burndown Charts**: Common in Agile projects, burndown charts illustrate work completed versus work remaining, helping teams visualize progress during sprints.
5. **Risk Registers**: Maintaining a risk register allows project managers to track identified risks, their potential impact, and the effectiveness of mitigation strategies.

Best Practices for Effective Monitoring and Control

1. **Establish Clear Metrics**: Define clear, measurable KPIs aligned with project objectives. These metrics should be communicated to all team members to ensure accountability.
2. **Regularly Review Progress**: Schedule regular progress reviews with the project team to assess performance and address any issues promptly. This could involve weekly or bi-weekly meetings to discuss status updates.
3. **Engage Stakeholders**: Keep stakeholders informed through regular updates and reports. Solicit their feedback and insights to enhance project outcomes and build trust.
4. **Be Proactive**: Adopt a proactive mindset toward monitoring and control. Anticipate potential

issues and develop contingency plans to address them.

5. **Encourage Team Collaboration**: Foster an environment of open communication and collaboration within the project team. Encourage team members to share concerns, challenges, and insights, enabling collective problem-solving.

6. **Document Changes**: Maintain thorough documentation of any changes to the project plan, including scope adjustments, timeline shifts, and budget alterations. This documentation provides a clear history of project decisions and actions.

Challenges in Project Monitoring and Control

1. **Data Overload**: With numerous data points to track, project managers may face information overload. It is essential to focus on the most relevant metrics that align with project objectives.

2. **Resistance to Change**: Team members may resist changes to the project plan or management processes. Effective communication and change management strategies are crucial for overcoming resistance.

3. **Limited Resources**: Constraints on time, personnel, or technology may hinder effective

monitoring. Prioritize key metrics and utilize available resources efficiently.
4. **Inconsistent Reporting**: Inconsistent reporting practices can lead to confusion and miscommunication. Establish standardized reporting templates and schedules to ensure uniformity.

Conclusion

Project monitoring and control are vital processes that enable project managers to ensure projects remain on track, within budget, and aligned with stakeholder expectations. By implementing effective monitoring strategies, utilizing appropriate tools, and fostering open communication, project managers can enhance project success and deliver value to stakeholders.

Chapter 15: Problem Solving and Decision Making

In project management, challenges and uncertainties are inevitable. Effective problem-solving and decision-making are crucial skills for project managers, enabling them to navigate obstacles, make informed choices, and steer projects toward success. This chapter will explore the principles and processes of problem-solving and decision-making, provide techniques and tools, and highlight the importance of collaboration and communication in these critical areas.

Understanding Problem Solving and Decision Making

Problem Solving involves identifying issues, analyzing potential causes, and developing solutions to address those issues. It is a systematic approach that seeks to resolve challenges that arise during a project, ensuring that objectives are met.

Decision Making is the process of selecting a course of action from multiple alternatives based on evaluation and analysis. It involves weighing the pros and cons of different options and considering their potential impact on project outcomes.

The Importance of Problem Solving and Decision Making

1. **Maintaining Project Momentum**: Effective problem-solving prevents minor issues from escalating into major setbacks, allowing projects to maintain their momentum and progress toward completion.
2. **Informed Choices**: Sound decision-making ensures that project managers choose the most viable options, balancing risks and benefits while aligning with project goals.
3. **Enhancing Team Collaboration**: Collaborative problem-solving fosters teamwork and creativity, bringing diverse perspectives and expertise to the table.
4. **Improving Project Outcomes**: By addressing issues promptly and making informed decisions, project managers can enhance project quality, reduce costs, and improve stakeholder satisfaction.

The Problem-Solving Process

1. **Identifying the Problem**: The first step in problem-solving is recognizing that an issue exists. This may involve gathering feedback from team members, monitoring project performance, or responding to stakeholder concerns.

2. **Defining the Problem**: Clearly define the problem by determining its scope and impact. Ask questions such as:
    - What are the symptoms of the problem?
    - Who is affected by it?
    - What are the potential consequences if it remains unresolved?
3. **Analyzing the Root Causes**: Conduct a thorough analysis to identify the underlying causes of the problem. Techniques such as the **5 Whys** or **Fishbone Diagram (Ishikawa)** can be effective for root cause analysis.
    - **5 Whys**: This technique involves asking "why" repeatedly (typically five times) until the root cause of the issue is identified.
    - **Fishbone Diagram**: This visual tool helps categorize potential causes of a problem, making it easier to identify root causes and contributing factors.
4. **Generating Solutions**: Brainstorm potential solutions to address the identified problem. Encourage creativity and open dialogue among team members to explore a wide range of ideas.
5. **Evaluating Alternatives**: Assess the feasibility, advantages, and disadvantages of each proposed solution. Consider factors such as cost, time, resources, and potential impact on project objectives.
6. **Selecting the Best Solution**: Choose the most viable solution based on the evaluation criteria.

Ensure that the selected option aligns with project goals and stakeholder expectations.

7. **Implementing the Solution**: Develop an action plan to implement the chosen solution. Assign responsibilities, set timelines, and allocate resources as needed to ensure effective execution.

8. **Monitoring and Reviewing**: After implementing the solution, monitor its effectiveness. Evaluate whether the problem has been resolved and if any new issues have emerged. Adjust the approach as necessary to achieve desired outcomes.

The Decision-Making Process

1. **Identifying the Decision**: Recognize that a decision needs to be made. This may arise from a change in project scope, resource availability, or stakeholder feedback.

2. **Gathering Information**: Collect relevant data and insights to inform the decision-making process. This may involve consulting with team members, analyzing performance metrics, or reviewing project documentation.

3. **Identifying Alternatives**: Generate a list of possible options or courses of action. Encourage diverse perspectives and input from team members to explore a range of alternatives.

4. **Evaluating Options**: Assess the pros and cons of each alternative. Consider potential impacts on project objectives, timelines, costs, and stakeholder interests. Techniques such as **SWOT Analysis** (Strengths, Weaknesses, Opportunities, Threats) can be beneficial in evaluating options.
5. **Making the Decision**: Select the best alternative based on the evaluation. Ensure that the chosen option aligns with project goals and is supported by stakeholders.
6. **Implementing the Decision**: Develop an action plan to implement the decision. Clearly communicate the plan to team members and assign responsibilities to ensure accountability.
7. **Monitoring Outcomes**: After implementation, monitor the outcomes of the decision. Evaluate whether it achieved the desired results and assess any unintended consequences.

Tools and Techniques for Problem Solving and Decision Making

1. **Brainstorming**: A collaborative technique that encourages the free flow of ideas. Participants share their thoughts without judgment, fostering creativity and innovation.
2. **Mind Mapping**: A visual tool that helps organize thoughts and ideas related to a problem or decision. It allows for the exploration of

connections and relationships between different concepts.

3. **Decision Trees**: A graphical representation of decisions and their possible consequences. Decision trees help visualize options and assess potential outcomes.

4. **Pros and Cons Lists**: A simple technique that involves listing the advantages and disadvantages of each option. This straightforward approach can clarify decision-making processes.

5. **Delphi Method**: A structured process that gathers input from a panel of experts through multiple rounds of anonymous feedback. This method helps achieve consensus on complex issues.

6. **Scenario Analysis**: A technique that evaluates potential future scenarios based on different decisions or actions. This approach helps project managers anticipate risks and plan for various outcomes.

Challenges in Problem Solving and Decision Making

1. **Biases**: Cognitive biases, such as confirmation bias or anchoring bias, can cloud judgment and lead to suboptimal decisions. Being aware of these biases is essential for objective decision-making.

2. **Time Constraints**: Tight deadlines may pressure project managers to make hasty decisions. Balancing speed with thoroughness is crucial for effective decision-making.
3. **Resistance to Change**: Team members may resist proposed solutions or decisions, particularly if they involve significant changes. Effective communication and change management strategies can help mitigate resistance.
4. **Information Overload**: The abundance of data and information can complicate decision-making processes. Prioritizing relevant information and focusing on key metrics can help alleviate this challenge.

Best Practices for Effective Problem Solving and Decision Making

1. **Encourage Collaboration**: Foster an environment where team members feel comfortable sharing ideas and perspectives. Diverse input leads to better problem-solving and decision-making outcomes.
2. **Communicate Clearly**: Ensure that communication is clear and concise, particularly when discussing problems and decisions. Transparency builds trust and encourages team buy-in.

3. **Document Processes**: Maintain thorough documentation of problem-solving and decision-making processes. This documentation provides a reference for future projects and helps track lessons learned.
4. **Reflect on Outcomes**: After resolving a problem or making a decision, take time to reflect on the outcomes. Evaluate what worked well and what could be improved for future situations.
5. **Stay Flexible**: Be prepared to adapt your approach as new information or circumstances arise. Flexibility is key to effective problem-solving and decision-making in a dynamic project environment.

Conclusion

Effective problem-solving and decision-making are critical skills for project managers, enabling them to navigate challenges, make informed choices, and drive projects toward successful outcomes. By following structured processes, leveraging collaborative techniques, and maintaining clear communication, project managers can enhance their ability to address issues and make decisions that align with project goals.

Chapter 16: Quality Management in Projects

Quality management is a vital aspect of project management, encompassing the processes and activities that ensure a project meets its defined quality standards and satisfies stakeholder expectations. This chapter will explore the principles and practices of quality management in projects, discuss the tools and techniques used to achieve quality, and highlight the importance of fostering a quality-centric culture within project teams.

Understanding Quality Management in Projects

Quality Management in projects involves three key processes: quality planning, quality assurance, and quality control. Each of these processes plays a crucial role in ensuring that project deliverables meet the required standards of quality.

1. **Quality Planning**: This process involves defining the quality standards relevant to the project and determining how those standards will be achieved. Quality planning sets the foundation for the entire quality management process and is closely linked to project scope and objectives.
2. **Quality Assurance (QA)**: QA refers to the systematic activities implemented within the

quality management system to ensure that quality requirements are met. It focuses on preventing defects and ensuring that the processes used in the project are effective and efficient.

3. **Quality Control (QC)**: QC is the process of monitoring and measuring project results to ensure that they meet the established quality standards. This involves regular inspections, testing, and evaluations to identify and correct any deficiencies.

The Importance of Quality Management

1. **Customer Satisfaction**: Delivering high-quality products and services enhances customer satisfaction and builds trust with stakeholders. Satisfied customers are more likely to become repeat clients and advocates for the project.

2. **Cost Efficiency**: Effective quality management reduces the likelihood of defects, rework, and delays, leading to cost savings and improved resource utilization. It helps avoid costly mistakes that can arise from poor quality.

3. **Reputation Management**: Consistently delivering quality results enhances the reputation of the project team and the organization. A strong reputation for quality can lead to more business opportunities and increased stakeholder confidence.

4. **Risk Mitigation**: Quality management identifies potential risks related to quality and provides strategies for mitigating those risks. This proactive approach helps prevent issues before they arise.

Key Components of Quality Management

1. **Quality Standards**: Establishing clear quality standards is crucial for effective quality management. These standards should align with industry benchmarks, regulatory requirements, and stakeholder expectations. Examples of quality standards include:
   - ISO 9001: A globally recognized standard for quality management systems.
   - Six Sigma: A methodology that focuses on reducing defects and improving processes.
   - Total Quality Management (TQM): A management approach centered on continuous improvement and customer satisfaction.

2. **Quality Metrics**: Defining specific quality metrics allows project managers to measure and evaluate quality performance. Common quality metrics include:
   - Defect density: The number of defects per unit of output.
   - Customer satisfaction scores: Measures of how well the project meets customer expectations.

- First-pass yield: The percentage of products that meet quality standards without rework.
3. **Quality Management Plan**: A comprehensive quality management plan outlines how quality will be managed throughout the project lifecycle. It includes:
    - Quality objectives and standards.
    - Roles and responsibilities for quality management.
    - Quality assurance and control processes.
    - Tools and techniques for measuring quality.

Tools and Techniques for Quality Management

1. **Quality Audits**: Conducting regular quality audits helps assess the effectiveness of quality management processes. Audits identify areas for improvement and ensure compliance with established quality standards.
2. **Process Mapping**: Mapping project processes allows teams to visualize workflows and identify potential areas for quality enhancement. Process mapping can help identify bottlenecks and inefficiencies that may impact quality.
3. **Checklists**: Utilizing checklists ensures that quality standards are consistently met throughout the project. Checklists provide a systematic approach for reviewing tasks and deliverables, helping to minimize errors.
4. **Root Cause Analysis (RCA)**: RCA is a problem-solving technique used to identify the underlying

causes of quality issues. Techniques such as the 5 Whys or Fishbone Diagram can help teams investigate quality problems and develop effective solutions.

5. **Control Charts**: Control charts are graphical representations that help monitor process performance over time. They enable project managers to detect variations in processes and assess whether they are within acceptable limits.

6. **Quality Improvement Programs**: Implementing quality improvement initiatives, such as Kaizen or Lean methodologies, promotes continuous improvement and fosters a culture of quality within the project team.

The Role of Leadership in Quality Management

Strong leadership is essential for fostering a culture of quality within project teams. Project managers should:

1. **Set Quality Expectations**: Clearly communicate quality expectations to the team and establish a commitment to quality at all levels.

2. **Empower Team Members**: Encourage team members to take ownership of quality by involving them in quality management processes and decision-making.

3. **Provide Training and Resources**: Invest in training and resources to equip team members

with the skills and knowledge necessary for effective quality management.

4. **Recognize and Reward Quality Efforts**: Acknowledge and celebrate team members' contributions to quality improvement initiatives. Recognizing quality efforts reinforces the importance of quality in the project.

Challenges in Quality Management

1. **Resistance to Change**: Team members may resist implementing quality management processes, particularly if they require significant changes to established workflows. Effective communication and change management strategies are essential for overcoming resistance.
2. **Resource Constraints**: Limited resources may hinder the ability to implement comprehensive quality management practices. Prioritizing quality initiatives and focusing on key metrics can help mitigate resource constraints.
3. **Complexity of Projects**: Complex projects with multiple stakeholders may present challenges in aligning quality standards and expectations. Establishing clear communication channels and stakeholder engagement strategies can help address these complexities.
4. **Balancing Quality and Time**: Project managers must balance the need for high-quality

deliverables with project timelines. Setting realistic quality objectives and timelines is crucial for achieving this balance.

Best Practices for Effective Quality Management

1. **Integrate Quality into Project Planning**: Include quality management as a core component of project planning. This ensures that quality considerations are incorporated into all phases of the project lifecycle.
2. **Foster a Quality Culture**: Encourage a culture of quality by promoting continuous improvement and empowering team members to take ownership of quality outcomes.
3. **Regularly Review Quality Metrics**: Monitor quality metrics throughout the project and conduct regular reviews to identify areas for improvement.
4. **Engage Stakeholders**: Involve stakeholders in the quality management process to gather feedback and align expectations. This collaboration enhances stakeholder satisfaction and promotes transparency.
5. **Document Lessons Learned**: Maintain documentation of quality-related lessons learned throughout the project. This documentation serves as a valuable resource for future projects and helps avoid repeating past mistakes.

Conclusion

Quality management is a critical aspect of project success, ensuring that deliverables meet established standards and satisfy stakeholder expectations. By implementing effective quality management processes, utilizing appropriate tools and techniques, and fostering a culture of quality, project managers can enhance project outcomes and drive continuous improvement.

Chapter 17: Handling Project Crisis and Recovery

Crisis situations can arise unexpectedly during any project, posing significant challenges that can threaten project success. The ability to effectively handle crises and navigate recovery is crucial for project managers. This chapter will explore the nature of project crises, strategies for crisis management, and the steps necessary for successful recovery, ensuring that projects can adapt and continue to meet their objectives.

Understanding Project Crises

A project crisis refers to any unforeseen event or situation that disrupts normal project operations and threatens the achievement of project goals. Crises can manifest in various forms, including:

- **Resource Shortages**: Sudden unavailability of key personnel or materials can hinder project progress.
- **Budget Overruns**: Unexpected costs can arise from scope changes, misestimations, or external factors, leading to budget crises.
- **Timeline Delays**: Delays caused by technical issues, regulatory changes, or stakeholder conflicts can jeopardize project schedules.
- **Stakeholder Conflicts**: Disagreements among stakeholders can escalate into crises, impacting decision-making and project direction.

- **Technical Failures**: Failures in technology or systems can halt project activities and require immediate resolution.

The Importance of Crisis Management

Effective crisis management is essential for several reasons:

1. **Minimizing Damage**: Quick and decisive action can help mitigate the impact of a crisis, reducing potential damage to the project, team morale, and stakeholder relationships.
2. **Maintaining Stakeholder Trust**: Transparent communication and proactive crisis management can help maintain stakeholder confidence, ensuring continued support for the project.
3. **Enhancing Resilience**: Learning to handle crises effectively builds organizational resilience, enabling teams to adapt to challenges and improve future project performance.
4. **Facilitating Recovery**: A structured approach to crisis management lays the groundwork for successful recovery, helping projects return to their original objectives.

The Crisis Management Process

1. **Crisis Identification**: The first step in crisis management is recognizing that a crisis exists.

This involves monitoring project performance, stakeholder feedback, and environmental changes to identify potential crises early.

2. **Assessment of Impact**: Once a crisis is identified, assess its impact on the project. Determine which aspects of the project are affected, including timelines, budgets, resources, and stakeholder relationships.

3. **Establishing a Crisis Management Team**: Form a dedicated crisis management team that includes key stakeholders and team members with relevant expertise. This team will be responsible for developing and implementing the crisis response plan.

4. **Developing a Crisis Response Plan**: Create a comprehensive crisis response plan that outlines the steps to address the crisis. Key elements of the plan include:
   - **Objectives**: Define the goals of the response, such as minimizing disruption or restoring stakeholder trust.
   - **Actions**: Specify the actions that will be taken to address the crisis, including short-term and long-term solutions.
   - **Responsibilities**: Assign roles and responsibilities to team members, ensuring that everyone understands their tasks in the crisis response.

5. **Communication Strategy**: Develop a communication strategy to keep stakeholders

informed throughout the crisis. Key considerations include:

- o **Transparency**: Be open about the nature of the crisis and the actions being taken to address it.
- o **Regular Updates**: Provide regular updates to stakeholders to keep them informed of progress and developments.
- o **Feedback Mechanism**: Establish channels for stakeholders to provide feedback and voice concerns, fostering a sense of collaboration.

6. **Implementation of the Response Plan**: Execute the crisis response plan, ensuring that team members are aware of their roles and responsibilities. Monitor progress closely and adjust actions as needed based on emerging information.

7. **Monitoring and Evaluation**: Continuously monitor the situation and evaluate the effectiveness of the crisis response. Gather data on key performance indicators (KPIs) to assess whether the crisis is being effectively managed.

8. **Adaptation and Improvement**: Be prepared to adapt the response as new information emerges. Flexibility is crucial in navigating crises, as circumstances may change rapidly.

Recovery Strategies

After addressing the immediate crisis, focus on recovery to restore the project to its original trajectory:

1. **Conduct a Post-Crisis Review**: Organize a post-crisis review to assess the effectiveness of the response and identify lessons learned. Discuss what worked well, what did not, and what improvements can be made for future crises.
2. **Reassess Project Objectives**: Evaluate whether the project's objectives need to be adjusted based on the impact of the crisis. Consider factors such as timelines, budgets, and stakeholder expectations.
3. **Engage Stakeholders**: Reconnect with stakeholders to rebuild trust and reinforce commitment to the project. Solicit their input on recovery efforts and incorporate their feedback into the recovery plan.
4. **Implement Corrective Actions**: Based on the findings from the post-crisis review, implement corrective actions to address any deficiencies in project processes or strategies. This may include revising risk management plans, updating quality standards, or enhancing communication protocols.
5. **Reinforce Team Morale**: Crises can impact team morale, so it is important to support team members during the recovery phase. Recognize their efforts, provide encouragement, and offer opportunities for team-building activities to restore a positive team dynamic.
6. **Strengthen Crisis Preparedness**: Use the lessons learned from the crisis to strengthen future crisis

preparedness. Develop or enhance crisis management training, update crisis response plans, and establish protocols for monitoring potential crises.

Tools and Techniques for Crisis Management

1. **Risk Management Framework**: Implement a robust risk management framework to identify, assess, and prioritize potential risks. Regularly review and update risk registers to ensure that emerging threats are addressed promptly.
2. **Crisis Simulations**: Conduct crisis simulations or tabletop exercises to prepare team members for potential crises. These exercises help identify weaknesses in crisis response plans and enhance team readiness.
3. **Communication Tools**: Utilize communication tools and platforms that facilitate quick and effective communication during crises. These tools can include messaging apps, project management software, and email alerts.
4. **Decision-Making Frameworks**: Establish decision-making frameworks to guide the crisis management team in making informed choices under pressure. Techniques such as SWOT analysis or multi-criteria decision analysis can help evaluate options.
5. **Monitoring Systems**: Implement monitoring systems that track project performance and

external factors. Real-time data can help identify potential crises early and enable proactive responses.

Challenges in Crisis Management

1. **Time Pressure**: Crises often require quick decision-making, which can lead to rushed or uninformed choices. Striking a balance between speed and thoroughness is crucial.
2. **Emotional Reactions**: Crises can trigger strong emotional responses from team members and stakeholders. Managing emotions and maintaining a calm and focused approach is essential for effective crisis management.
3. **Complex Stakeholder Dynamics**: Diverse stakeholder interests can complicate crisis management efforts. Navigating these dynamics while maintaining transparency and collaboration is key.
4. **Limited Resources**: Crises may strain available resources, making it challenging to implement effective responses. Prioritizing critical actions and leveraging existing resources is essential.

Best Practices for Effective Crisis Management

1. **Be Proactive**: Anticipate potential crises and establish preventive measures. A proactive

approach can help mitigate risks and minimize the likelihood of crises occurring.

2. **Maintain Open Communication**: Foster a culture of open communication where team members feel comfortable raising concerns. Early identification of issues can prevent crises from escalating.

3. **Build Strong Relationships**: Cultivating strong relationships with stakeholders enhances trust and collaboration, making it easier to navigate crises together.

4. **Document Lessons Learned**: Maintain thorough documentation of crisis events, responses, and lessons learned. This documentation serves as a valuable resource for improving future crisis management efforts.

5. **Regularly Review Crisis Plans**: Periodically review and update crisis management plans to ensure they remain relevant and effective. Involve team members in these reviews to incorporate diverse perspectives.

Conclusion

Handling project crises effectively is a critical skill for project managers, enabling them to navigate challenges and facilitate recovery. By implementing structured crisis management processes, fostering a culture of communication and collaboration, and learning from experiences, project managers can enhance their ability to address crises and guide projects toward success. In the next chapter, we will explore project closure and evaluation, focusing on best practices for concluding projects successfully and capturing lessons learned for future initiatives.

Chapter 18: Closing Projects Successfully

The closing phase of a project is critical for ensuring that all aspects of the project are finalized, and that lessons learned are documented for future reference. A successful project closure not only marks the official end of the project but also sets the stage for future initiatives by providing valuable insights and a sense of accomplishment. This chapter will outline the essential components of successful project closure, including processes, documentation, and stakeholder engagement.

Understanding Project Closure

Project closure refers to the formal conclusion of all project activities. This phase includes the completion of project deliverables, release of project resources, and evaluation of project outcomes. Closing a project successfully involves more than just finishing tasks; it requires a structured approach to ensure that everything is wrapped up properly and stakeholders are satisfied.

Importance of Project Closure

1. **Ensures Completion of Deliverables**: Closing the project helps confirm that all deliverables have

been completed to the required standards and meet stakeholder expectations.

2. **Facilitates Resource Release**: Officially closing the project allows for the release of team members and resources, enabling them to be reassigned to new initiatives.

3. **Enhances Learning and Improvement**: A thorough project closure process captures lessons learned, providing insights for improving future projects and avoiding past mistakes.

4. **Strengthens Stakeholder Relationships**: Proper closure ensures that stakeholders feel valued and informed, enhancing trust and collaboration for future endeavors.

5. **Provides a Sense of Achievement**: Successfully closing a project instills a sense of accomplishment within the team and stakeholders, reinforcing motivation for future projects.

Key Steps in Project Closure

1. **Final Deliverables and Acceptance**:
   o Ensure that all project deliverables are completed and meet the predefined quality standards.
   o Conduct a formal acceptance process with stakeholders to obtain their approval and sign-off on the deliverables. This may involve presentations, demonstrations, or review sessions.

2. **Documentation of Project Results**:
   - o Compile comprehensive documentation that outlines project outcomes, including performance against objectives, budget adherence, and timeline compliance.
   - o Create a project closure report that summarizes key achievements, challenges faced, and how they were addressed. This report serves as a valuable reference for future projects.
3. **Release of Resources**:
   - o Plan for the systematic release of project resources, including team members, equipment, and budget allocations.
   - o Conduct exit interviews with team members to gather feedback and assess their experiences during the project.
4. **Conducting a Post-Project Review**:
   - o Organize a post-project review meeting with key stakeholders and team members. Discuss what went well, what didn't, and identify lessons learned.
   - o Use structured techniques, such as SWOT analysis (Strengths, Weaknesses, Opportunities, Threats), to facilitate discussions and gather insights.
5. **Capturing Lessons Learned**:
   - o Document lessons learned throughout the project and during the closure phase. This can include insights related to processes, team dynamics, stakeholder engagement, and risk management.

- Create a lessons learned repository that can be referenced by future project teams, fostering a culture of continuous improvement.

6. **Formal Closure and Celebration**:
    - Prepare for a formal project closure, which may include a closing ceremony or event to celebrate achievements and recognize team efforts.
    - Acknowledge individual contributions and provide positive reinforcement to strengthen team morale.

7. **Communicating Closure to Stakeholders**:
    - Inform all stakeholders of the project's closure through formal communication channels, such as emails, newsletters, or meetings.
    - Share highlights from the project, including key achievements, lessons learned, and the impact of the project on the organization or community.

8. **Archiving Project Documentation**:
    - Organize and archive all project documentation, including project plans, reports, contracts, and correspondence. Ensure that these documents are easily accessible for future reference.
    - Consider using a centralized document management system to store project records and maintain organization.

Best Practices for Closing Projects Successfully

1. **Plan for Closure from the Beginning**:
   o Incorporate project closure activities into the project plan from the outset. This ensures that closure is not overlooked and allows for smoother transitions at the end of the project.

2. **Engage Stakeholders Early**:
   o Involve stakeholders in the closure process by seeking their input and feedback throughout the project. This helps ensure that their expectations are met and that they feel included in the closing activities.

3. **Be Thorough and Detailed**:
   o Pay attention to detail during the closure phase. Ensure that all deliverables, documentation, and processes are completed comprehensively to avoid overlooking critical elements.

4. **Foster Open Communication**:
   o Maintain transparent communication with team members and stakeholders throughout the closure process. Encourage questions, discussions, and feedback to create an inclusive environment.

5. **Use Technology to Support Closure**:
   o Leverage project management tools and software to streamline closure activities. These tools can help track completion of tasks, document lessons learned, and facilitate communication.

6. **Evaluate Team Performance**:
    o   Assess team performance throughout the project and during the closure phase. Provide constructive feedback to individuals and recognize achievements to enhance professional development.

Challenges in Project Closure

1. **Unresolved Issues**:
    o   Some projects may face unresolved issues or incomplete deliverables at the time of closure. It is essential to address these concerns and develop a plan for follow-up actions.
2. **Resistance to Closure**:
    o   Team members may experience resistance to closure, particularly if they are emotionally invested in the project. Acknowledging their feelings and providing support can help ease the transition.
3. **Time Constraints**:
    o   Project closure can be rushed due to time constraints or pressure to move on to new initiatives. Prioritizing closure activities is essential to ensure thoroughness.
4. **Limited Stakeholder Engagement**:
    o   Some stakeholders may disengage during the closure phase, making it challenging to gather feedback or achieve acceptance. Actively engaging stakeholders throughout the closure process can mitigate this risk.

Conclusion

Closing projects successfully is a vital aspect of project management that requires careful planning, thorough documentation, and effective communication. By following a structured approach to project closure, project managers can ensure that all deliverables are completed, resources are appropriately released, and valuable lessons are captured for future endeavors. In the next chapter, we will explore the importance of continuous improvement in project management, focusing on strategies to enhance project performance over time.

Chapter 19: Lessons Learned and Continuous Improvement

In the realm of project management, the concept of "lessons learned" plays a crucial role in driving future success. Each project, regardless of its outcome, offers valuable insights that can be leveraged to improve processes, enhance team performance, and increase stakeholder satisfaction in future endeavors. This chapter delves into the importance of documenting lessons learned, the processes involved, and the strategies for fostering a culture of continuous improvement within an organization.

Understanding Lessons Learned

Lessons learned refer to the knowledge gained from the experience of conducting a project. This can include insights related to successes, challenges, and the overall project experience. By systematically capturing and analyzing these lessons, project managers and teams can identify areas for improvement, refine their practices, and make informed decisions in future projects.

The Importance of Lessons Learned

1. **Enhances Project Performance**: Documenting lessons learned helps identify what worked well

and what did not, enabling teams to replicate successes and avoid repeating mistakes in future projects.

2. **Fosters Knowledge Sharing**: A centralized repository of lessons learned promotes knowledge sharing across the organization, ensuring that valuable insights are accessible to all team members and project managers.

3. **Supports Risk Management**: By analyzing past experiences, project teams can better anticipate and mitigate risks in future projects, leading to improved project outcomes.

4. **Encourages Accountability**: The process of documenting lessons learned instills a sense of accountability within project teams, encouraging them to reflect on their performance and seek continuous improvement.

5. **Improves Stakeholder Satisfaction**: By implementing lessons learned, organizations can enhance their service delivery, leading to greater stakeholder satisfaction and loyalty.

The Lessons Learned Process

1. **Identify Lessons Learned**:
   o Throughout the project lifecycle, team members should be encouraged to document lessons learned as they arise. This can be done through informal discussions, team meetings, and project documentation.

- o Utilize specific prompts, such as "What went well?" and "What could have been done better?" to facilitate discussions and ensure comprehensive coverage of experiences.

2. **Gather Feedback**:
   - o Conduct post-project review meetings with team members and stakeholders to gather feedback on the project's execution. Use structured techniques, such as surveys or SWOT analysis, to encourage open and honest dialogue.
   - o Consider conducting one-on-one interviews with key stakeholders to gather in-depth insights and perspectives.

3. **Document Lessons Learned**:
   - o Compile and categorize the identified lessons learned into a centralized repository. This can be in the form of a lessons learned database or a dedicated section in the project closure report.
   - o Clearly outline each lesson learned, its context, implications, and recommendations for future projects. Use specific examples to illustrate points and enhance understanding.

4. **Analyze Lessons Learned**:
   - o Review the documented lessons learned to identify patterns and trends that can inform future projects. Consider conducting a root cause analysis for significant issues to understand underlying causes and develop strategies for mitigation.
   - o Engage the project team in discussions to brainstorm potential solutions and

improvements based on the analyzed lessons.

5. **Implement Improvements**:
   - o Develop action plans to implement the recommendations derived from lessons learned. Assign responsibilities and set timelines for executing these improvements in future projects.
   - o Communicate the action plans to all relevant stakeholders to ensure alignment and accountability.

6. **Review and Update**:
   - o Regularly review and update the lessons learned repository to ensure it remains relevant and reflects the organization's evolving practices and experiences.
   - o Encourage ongoing contributions to the repository by fostering a culture of continuous improvement and knowledge sharing.

Fostering a Culture of Continuous Improvement

1. **Leadership Support**:
   - o Leadership plays a crucial role in promoting a culture of continuous improvement. Leaders should encourage open communication, recognize contributions, and demonstrate a commitment to learning and growth.
   - o Provide resources and training to equip teams with the skills and knowledge needed to implement lessons learned effectively.

2. **Encourage Collaboration**:
   - Foster collaboration among project teams to share experiences and insights. Establish cross-functional teams or communities of practice to facilitate knowledge exchange and collective learning.
   - Implement regular forums, such as lunch-and-learn sessions or workshops, to discuss lessons learned and improvement opportunities.

3. **Emphasize Training and Development**:
   - Invest in training programs that focus on project management best practices, risk management, and team dynamics. This ensures that team members are equipped with the latest knowledge and skills to enhance project performance.
   - Incorporate lessons learned into training materials and onboarding processes for new team members.

4. **Measure Success**:
   - Establish key performance indicators (KPIs) to assess the impact of implemented improvements. This allows organizations to track progress and identify areas for further enhancement.
   - Conduct regular reviews to evaluate the effectiveness of changes made based on lessons learned and adjust strategies as needed.

5. **Create a Feedback Loop**:
   - Implement mechanisms for ongoing feedback from team members and

stakeholders throughout the project lifecycle. This ensures that lessons learned are continuously integrated into current practices and informs decision-making.
- o Encourage teams to regularly reflect on their experiences and share insights in real-time, rather than waiting for the project closure phase.

Challenges in Implementing Lessons Learned

1. **Resistance to Change**:
   - o Some team members may resist changes based on lessons learned due to fear of disrupting established processes or uncertainty about new approaches. Addressing these concerns through clear communication and demonstrating the benefits of change can help mitigate resistance.
2. **Lack of Time**:
   - o Project teams often face time constraints that may hinder their ability to document and analyze lessons learned. Allocating dedicated time for reflection and discussion during project meetings can help prioritize this important process.
3. **Limited Engagement**:
   - o Team members may not engage fully in the lessons learned process if they feel their input is not valued or considered. Encouraging participation and recognizing

contributions can foster a more collaborative environment.

4. **Inconsistent Documentation**:
    o   Variability in how lessons learned are documented across projects can lead to confusion and inefficiency. Establishing standardized templates and processes for documenting lessons learned can promote consistency and clarity.

Conclusion

The documentation of lessons learned and the commitment to continuous improvement are fundamental to successful project management. By capturing insights from past experiences, organizations can enhance project performance, foster a culture of learning, and improve stakeholder satisfaction. In the final chapter, we will explore the future of project management, focusing on emerging trends and technologies that are shaping the discipline.

Chapter 20: The Future of Project Management

As the landscape of business and technology continues to evolve, so too does the field of project management. The future of project management will be shaped by emerging trends, evolving methodologies, and the increasing complexity of projects across various industries. In this chapter, we will explore the key drivers of change in project management, the implications of these changes, and the skills and tools necessary for project managers to thrive in this dynamic environment.

Key Drivers of Change in Project Management

1. **Technological Advancements**:
    - Rapid advancements in technology, such as artificial intelligence (AI), machine learning, big data analytics, and cloud computing, are transforming how projects are planned, executed, and monitored.
    - Tools powered by AI can analyze large datasets to provide insights into project performance, predict potential risks, and recommend optimal resource allocation, enabling project managers to make data-driven decisions.

2. **Agile and Hybrid Methodologies**:
   - The shift towards agile methodologies has revolutionized project management, promoting flexibility, collaboration, and iterative development. Agile frameworks allow teams to adapt quickly to changing requirements and deliver incremental value to stakeholders.
   - Many organizations are now adopting hybrid project management approaches, which combine elements of traditional and agile methodologies to suit specific project needs. This trend emphasizes the importance of tailoring methodologies to fit the unique characteristics of each project.

3. **Remote and Distributed Teams**:
   - The rise of remote work and distributed teams has fundamentally altered the way projects are managed. Project managers must navigate the challenges of coordinating teams across different locations, time zones, and cultures.
   - Effective communication, collaboration tools, and a focus on building a strong team culture are essential for managing remote teams successfully.

4. **Emphasis on Soft Skills**:
   - As projects become increasingly complex, the importance of soft skills, such as emotional intelligence, communication, and conflict resolution, is gaining recognition. Project managers must cultivate these skills to lead

diverse teams and navigate interpersonal dynamics effectively.

- The ability to build relationships and foster collaboration among team members and stakeholders is crucial for project success in the future.

5. **Sustainability and Social Responsibility**:
    - Growing awareness of environmental and social issues is driving organizations to adopt sustainable practices in project management. This includes considering the long-term impacts of projects on communities, the environment, and stakeholders.
    - Project managers will need to incorporate sustainability principles into project planning and execution, ensuring that projects align with organizational values and societal expectations.

Implications for Project Managers

1. **Adapting to New Technologies**:
    - Project managers must stay abreast of emerging technologies and trends to leverage them effectively in their projects. Continuous learning and professional development will be essential to remain competitive in the evolving landscape.
    - Familiarity with project management software, collaboration tools, and data analytics platforms will become increasingly important for project managers.

2. **Embracing Agility**:
   - o   To thrive in a fast-paced environment, project managers should embrace agility not only in project methodologies but also in their mindset. This includes being open to change, encouraging experimentation, and fostering a culture of continuous improvement.
   - o   Project managers will need to balance the need for structure with the flexibility to adapt to evolving circumstances and stakeholder needs.

3. **Strengthening Communication Skills**:
   - o   As remote and distributed teams become the norm, effective communication skills will be paramount. Project managers should prioritize clear, concise, and transparent communication with team members and stakeholders.
   - o   Utilizing a variety of communication channels, including virtual meetings, collaboration platforms, and project management tools, can enhance engagement and collaboration among team members.

4. **Cultivating Emotional Intelligence**:
   - o   Developing emotional intelligence will be crucial for project managers to understand team dynamics, address conflicts, and motivate team members effectively. Project managers should focus on building strong relationships and fostering a supportive team environment.

- Recognizing and managing their own emotions, as well as those of others, will help project managers navigate challenges and enhance team performance.

5. **Integrating Sustainability Practices**:
   - Project managers will increasingly need to incorporate sustainability considerations into their project planning and decision-making processes. This may involve conducting sustainability assessments, setting sustainability goals, and engaging stakeholders in discussions about environmental impacts.
   - Understanding the principles of sustainable project management will be vital for aligning projects with organizational goals and societal expectations.

Tools and Technologies Shaping the Future of Project Management

1. **Project Management Software**:
   - The future of project management will be heavily influenced by advanced project management software that incorporates AI, automation, and real-time collaboration features. Tools such as Asana, Trello, and Microsoft Project are evolving to support remote teams and facilitate agile project management.
   - These tools enable project managers to track progress, allocate resources, and

communicate effectively with team members in real-time.

2. **Collaboration Platforms**:
   o The rise of collaboration platforms, such as Slack, Microsoft Teams, and Zoom, is changing the way project teams communicate and work together. These platforms provide instant messaging, video conferencing, and file sharing capabilities, fostering seamless collaboration among distributed teams.
   o Integrating collaboration tools with project management software can enhance efficiency and streamline workflows.

3. **Data Analytics and Business Intelligence**:
   o Data analytics tools are becoming essential for project managers to gain insights into project performance, identify trends, and make informed decisions. Tools like Tableau and Power BI enable project managers to visualize data and track key performance indicators (KPIs).
   o By leveraging data analytics, project managers can proactively address potential issues and optimize project outcomes.

4. **Artificial Intelligence and Machine Learning**:
   o AI and machine learning technologies are transforming project management by automating repetitive tasks, predicting project risks, and providing actionable insights. AI-powered tools can analyze historical project data to identify patterns

and suggest improvements for future projects.

- o Project managers can utilize AI to enhance decision-making, improve resource allocation, and streamline processes.

5. **Virtual and Augmented Reality**:
   - o Virtual and augmented reality technologies are beginning to make their mark in project management, particularly in industries such as construction, engineering, and training. These technologies can provide immersive simulations, enabling project managers and teams to visualize project designs and identify potential issues before implementation.
   - o Integrating VR and AR into project management processes can enhance collaboration and improve stakeholder engagement.

Conclusion

The future of project management is poised for transformation, driven by technological advancements, evolving methodologies, and a focus on sustainability and soft skills. Project managers must adapt to these changes by embracing new technologies, cultivating essential skills, and fostering a culture of continuous improvement. By doing so, they can navigate the complexities of modern projects and lead their teams to success in an ever-changing landscape.

In conclusion, as we reflect on the key concepts covered in this handbook, it is clear that project management is not merely a set of processes but a dynamic discipline that requires adaptability, innovation, and a commitment to learning. By applying the principles outlined in this book, project managers can enhance their effectiveness and drive successful outcomes for their projects and organizations. The journey of project management is ongoing, and with each project, there lies an opportunity for growth, improvement, and achievement.